"Fresh from the Kitchen"

Life Lessons of a Big Dreamer

3rd Edition - 2020

Frank C. Kitchen

Published by Frank Kitchen Enterprises. LLC, 500 N. Estrella Parkway, Suite B2137, Goodyear, AZ 85338 www.FrankKitchen.com

THANK YOU FOR SUPPORTING CMCA!

Live FRESH!

"Fresh from the Kitchen"

Significant portions of this book this book first appeared in some format,
on the blogs at:

www.kitchenfrank.blogspot.com
and
www.frankkitchen.com

Manufactured in the United States of America. ISBN: 9781656194138

Cover Photo by Mitchell Brown www.facesofmitchell.com

Table of Contents

44 Lessons for Cooking Up the Dreams You Hunger For

Table of Contents

44 Life Lessons for Personal & Professional Growth

"Fresh from the Kitchen"

Forward

By Rodger N. Campbell

Like a bolt of lightning in the evening sky, inspiration strikes with power, brightens the world, and powerfully energizes everything in its path. It can surge while you quietly watch an evening sunset at the beach. It can pulse during the drive home from work while listening to your favorite song. It can explode while you're at home with friends, enjoying a meal fresh from the kitchen. Inspiration strikes when you least expect it, but just when it is needed. You picked up this book because the time is right for inspiration.

Wherever he is, Frank Kitchen is that inspirational bolt of lighting. He brightens the world with his passion to serve, and powerfully energizes with his wit and encouragement. For over two decades, I've experienced Frank's wit and candor. His quiet demeanor masks his sharp insight, which he shares in his unique story-telling style. His life has been a winding journey full of ups and downs, twists and turns, giving him well-seasoned stories rich with the full flavor of real life. Watching him pursue his dream with a steady resolve has inspired and challenged me just to keep up.

"Fresh from the Kitchen"

In this book, you too will be exposed to Frank's humor, insight, but most of all his heart. Helping individuals believe in themselves and their dreams is his passion. He possesses the uncanny ability to put light on an obvious subject, which transcends the surface and gets to the core of the matter. He's often said: "I might not be the smartest person in the world, but I have eyes." I think he's just being humble. Without a doubt, Frank has big eyes with extremely keen vision. He will challenge you to look beyond what you think you see to view what is really there...possibilities. His fresh ideas are hot, like a good meal, and just as filling. Your stomach will be full of laughter and your heart warmed, the sign of a great meal. Grab a comfy chair, get your cozy blanket, sit back and enjoy the "culinary" delights Frank has whipped up for you. Some stories might be a bit "hot," but you'll always know it is Fresh from the Kitchen.

Acknowledgments

Dear Family, Friends, and Readers,

I would like to thank you for investing in my book and my career. Without your support, the lessons shared in this book would not be possible. Life is about relationships, experiences and lessons learned. The relationships I have cultivated have allowed me to share my experiences both positive and negative with you in this book.

There were a lot of people who played roles in the writing of this 3rd edition "Fresh from the Kitchen." I would live to acknowledge them now.

My wife Kelly is the amazing woman that I am forever indebted to. Her physical, fiscal, and emotional support gave me the motivation I needed to pursue this experience. I am truly blessed to have her in my life. Thank you, *AGP,* for sharing your life with me.

My kids, Elijah and Olivia are a constant motivation to keep doing what I do. They weren't around when I wrote the first edition of this book, but they are very much the reason why I've become a better leader and person.

Rodger Campbell is my big brother, coach, mentor, business partner, and friend. His constant prodding is one of the reasons I wrote this book and had the courage to step out on my own.

"Fresh from the Kitchen"

Thank you, *Doctor Campbell,* for providing me with the medicine to be *SumThing Else.*

Scott Cummings in my best friend and someone I truly look up to. He is a role model who provides me with constant encouragement. His recommendation for a speech in 2015 was the catalyst to reignite my speaking career. Thank you, *Skillz,* for always being there for the good times and the not so good times.

Melissa Kitchen is my sister and Ms. Honesty. I know that I can always go to her for an honest opinion. She has always believed in me and given me great ideas and advice. Thank you, *Mimi;* you are an amazing woman. Your passion always inspires me.

David and Judy Duran. Your support and trust during my down times kept my dream alive and our family afloat. Thank you!

To all of my friends around the world, especially the ones from Ohio who I call family...Thank you for keeping my head on straight and treating me like family.

Finally, Edie Mack, my mom. To my biggest fan, you are the reason that I am the man I am today. You are a teacher in real life, and my teacher for life. Thank you, Mom, for teaching me everything you know! Many of the lessons I am sharing in this book were ideas you first planted in me.

Writing this book has been a decade long experience. I truly hope you enjoy what you read inside. - ***Frank***

Lesson 1

"People want to Know You and Your Story!"

A blog is defined as a website written by an individual or group of users to produce an ongoing narrative. It comes from the words web and log.

A book is defined as a written piece of work consisting of pages glued or sewn together and bound by a cover.

Throughout my life, people have told me I should write a book to share my adventures, knowledge and the lessons I have learned along the way. I thought that it was weird, considering I have no formal journalistic training. I wasn't an avid reader of books. I wasn't a fan of writing long papers in school. How was I going to write a book?

My mom made me read a lot as a child. She signed me up for the *Weekly Reader Book Club.* Every week, a new book came in the mail. I read the ones that I liked, while many went unread. Most of my reading encompassed comic books, the world atlas, magazines, and advertisements.

Then, I graduated from college and entered the professional workplace. I needed to share my thoughts with others when I couldn't share them verbally. I started writing newsletters. It was an easy and fun way to share important information.

I could put my thoughts together in a clear and concise way. I could be direct and to the point without writing a book.

In the summer of 2005, my immediate family moved away to Florida. I wanted them to keep up to date with my life in Ohio. That's when I was introduced to the world of blogging. A friend showed me how to set up my own site. Soon, I was posting stories and pictures of my life's ups and downs. My family and friends could see what I was up to. I named my blog "Fresh from the Kitchen." Every entry was a fresh idea that I could share with the people close to me. Before I knew it, people I didn't know were reading my blog.

People enjoyed my thoughts and ideas on a variety of subjects. They were sharing them with their family and friends. I wrote a blog while I was in Australia and discovered that people were reading my blog daily with their morning coffee. There were people who sent me concerned emails when I didn't blog for an extended period of time. There were even more people who commented that I should write a book.

Still, writing a book seemed impossible. I told myself that I didn't have time to write a book. I made excuses about being too busy. I was too busy living life and sharing the stories on my blog. One night while uploading a new blog entry, I began reading my past entries. There were over 600 entries to sort through. I discovered that I had enough material to write several books.

That is the night my idea light bulb lit up above my head*: write your book like you write your blogs! Write a narrative of stories bound by a cover.* People write books for many reasons. My reason is simple: I would like to share lessons that will educate, elevate and empower people to live their personal and professional dreams.

To read my past and current blogs, please visit:

www.kitchenfrank.blogspot.com

www.frankkitchen.com/blog

Lesson 2

"Life is about Experiences and Relationships."

"Life is about experiences and relationships!" – Bernie Morgan

In 2006, I was sitting in the home of Bernie Morgan in Adelaide, Australia. I was having an insightful conversation with Bernie, his wife Colleen, and my friend Dave. We discussed politics, religion, family, friends, food, and wine. While sipping a glass of wine, Bernie made the quote that has changed my life. *Life is about experiences and relationships.*

I was in Australia for the adventure of a lifetime. Six weeks exploring the country as representative for Rotary International and the United States. Bernie and his wife Colleen were hosting my friend Dave and I. As our host family, they taught us about their country and culture. Bernie and Colleen aren't big fans of television. They are big fans of developing strong relationships and creating lasting memories. The week that I spent with them was amazing.

Time spent with Bernie and Colleen was all about people. It was about learning and communication. It was about experiences. One of my experiences took place on Easter Sunday. Bernie took our group to a hanger at a small airfield. The hanger belonged to a friend who collected vintage aircraft.

One of his prized planes was a World War I United States Army biplane. Our group of three each had the opportunity to fly in the plane.

I was the last person to fly in the open cockpit plane. The weather was perfect, the views were amazing, and the experience is permanently etched in my mind and the digital folder of my computer marked, "Australia Trip."

Reliving that story made me realize that I have an amazing life. I've accomplished more than I could have imagined. I have been told my stories and experiences are inspiring. Truth be told, they inspire me too. They give me the urge to pursue new experiences and to continue to develop positive relationships. The stories of these experiences and relationships will be shared with you in this book.

Amazing experiences are the offspring of strong and positive relationships. You too have lived an amazing life. You have and will accomplish the unthinkable. Your experiences can inspire the people around you. They will inspire you to do more in the future. Life is a celebration. Make time to relive your accomplishments. Dedicate time to develop and nurture relationships. Make the most out of every experience. And, remember to celebrate!

Thank you, Bernie and Colleen, for a very important life lesson and your continued friendship.

Lesson 3

"Listen to the Advice Special People Offer to You."

"Really great people make you feel that you, too can become great." – Mark Twain

I worked at Lakeland Community College in Kirtland, Ohio for nine years. I left the school in July of 2007 to pursue a career as a professional speaker, and to move closer to my future wife, Kelly, in Arizona. Many of my coworkers and students told me that they would miss me.

I informed the college of my decision to leave that May. Every week, the President of the Lakeland would send out a letter (email) to the employees. The email would cover a variety of subjects. That May, he asked college employees to contribute to his weekly email. When word of my departure spread, he asked me to write something. Here's what I wrote. This is one of the *light bulb* moments that made me write this book.

(May 2007)

I received a phone call last week from the President's Office "asking" me if I would write the next edition of "Morris' Musings." My options were "yes" or "yes." I decided on option number two. Once I committed myself to be this week's "Special Guest Writer," I needed something to write about.

“Fresh from the Kitchen”

Should I write something serious? Should I be funny? Should I keep it short? Hmmmm? Then it hit me: I’m going to do what I do best, I’m going to be me! First step, name my musing. “Fresh from the Kitchen.” Next step, start typing.

“Fresh from the Kitchen” Edition #1

Friday, July 20, 2007 will be my last day of employment at Lakeland Community College. My experiences at Lakeland have been amazing. I often tell people that I might have to write a book or a sitcom about some of the experiences. We often refer to the people who work here as “The Lakeland Family.” I would like to thank that family for taking me in. I especially want to thank Rich Novotny for taking the chance to hire and mentor an inexperienced kid nine years ago.

That leads me to my musing. I would like to thank Morris for inviting me to write to all of you. I also want to thank Morris in advance for the Clocktower Award presented to me for all my hard work on this musing (hint, hint). I’ve been reading Morris’ Musings since he started writing them. At the end of every musing, he thanks everyone for Impacting Lives through Learning. I often think to myself, what does that mean? “Impacting Lives through Learning” is Lakeland’s slogan. It’s Lakeland's core purpose. Do we think about this core purpose every time we come to Lakeland?

"Fresh from the Kitchen"

In December of 1991, I moved to Mentor, Ohio from Philadelphia, Pennsylvania. I had the grades, several college acceptance letters, but not enough money to go to the "REAL" colleges.

My mom suggested I enroll at Lakeland Community College. I was a little hesitant at first. I didn't want to go to a "community college"!
I will admit, I was very young and very misinformed about community colleges. In 1992, I started taking classes at Lakeland. I soon discovered how much of an impact Lakeland would have on my life.

Impact is defined as a significant or strong influence. It is also defined as the effect something has on something else. This influence or effect can be positive or negative. In my case, the impact was very positive. As a student, Lakeland offered affordable classes taught by top-notch instructors. Lakeland also offered a variety of co-curricular opportunities to help me grow personally outside the classroom. That combination turned a shy kid into an outgoing young adult with a two-year Associates Degree in 1995.

I eventually transferred to the University of Akron, then went on to Myers University. Then, I got my first job in the real world. At school or at work, I was often asked, "Where did you learn that?" I always replied, "Lakeland Community College." I started to recognize how much of an impact Lakeland had on my life. It was more personal than the real schools.

I could talk to someone face to face when I needed help or assistance. I learned skills for the classroom, and skills for life, from the people at Lakeland.

I eventually came back to Lakeland in 1998 to work in the Student Activities Office. What a great opportunity and experience! I wanted to share the positive experiences that I had as a Lakeland student with current students.

Many students and their parents tell me about the positive impact Lakeland and I had on their lives. Many of those students don't realize the impact they have on my life and our lives. They help us as we continue to learn and grow.

Fifteen years after I first stepped foot on the Lakeland campus, I am preparing to leave again. I'm preparing to take on the new challenge of living in a new state, developing new relationships and pursuing new career opportunities. I start to think what got me to this point and once again I know its Lakeland. There is a statement: "you never know what you have until it's gone." Soon Lakeland will be a memory, but I'll always remember my time here.

Being in a learning environment is motivating. Everyone has a dream. Everyone wants to take on the world in some way. Lakeland is a stepping-stone for students to achieve their dreams. The faculty and staff at Lakeland have a strong influence on students achieving their dreams. We are the "something" affecting "something" else.

"Fresh from the Kitchen"

We are all here because of the students. Without the students, we wouldn't have our jobs. Every time a student or prospective student comes in contact with a member of the Lakeland Family, we are impacting their lives. Learning doesn't only happen in the classroom, it happens everywhere on campus. We need to think about how we can impact the lives of the students and our Lakeland Family members in a positive way

Do you know who's who on campus? Do you know the responsibilities of the different departments? If you see trash around campus, do you pick it up? Do you answer your phone or let it go into voicemail? Do you complain about everything or make suggestions for improvement? Do you respond quickly to your emails? Do you help mentor new college employees? Do you attend campus events or programs? Do you take advantage of the classes offered? Do you share your Lakeland stories with students and co-workers? The list goes on and on. All are examples of experiences that impact people (students and employees) on campus. We have the choice to make it a positive or negative experience. That choice impacts the lives of many people: prospective students, current students, and employees.

Lakeland has used the slogans "Students First," "Opportunity Starts Here," and currently "Impacting Lives through Learning." These words focus on the number one thing at Lakeland: the students. Lakeland and its employees have had a positive impact on thousands of students/people. I am one of them. In turn, I have positively impacted the lives of others.

"Fresh from the Kitchen"

It's easy to focus on the negative, but we should take the time to focus on the positive impact we can make. The next time you read Morris's Musing and you see the term "Impacting Lives through Learning," think about that new student stepping on campus for the first time or that student crossing the stage at graduation. Think about what you do here at Lakeland. Ask yourself: "Does my attitude or work make a negative impact on that life or a positive impact?" I hope all of you go for option number two! Thank you, Lakeland, Frank Kitchen

A few days later, I received this email and advice from Dr. Morris W. Beverage, Jr, President of Lakeland Community College:

Frank,

It looks like you may be onto something here. You could start by simply doing a personal journal. Then, after a few years, you could publish your writings and retire a wealthy and young man. Then, you could come back here and be President. Just something to think about. Thanks again, Frank. I would say your Kitchen Musing was very well-received.

Morris

Lesson 4

"Invest in a Journal."

"Fill your paper with the breathings of your heart."
– William Wordsworth

My wife has given me wonderful gifts over the years. One of the best gifts she ever gave me was a journal. When I started writing this book, I began to look for ideas and inspiration. "What will I write about?" "Shouldn't it be called typing a book, not writing?" How will I communicate my feelings?" I immediately went to my journal. My journal is the place where I write down all of my dreams and quotes that inspire me to accomplish my dreams. While going through my journal, I came across three entries:

"What do you believe in?" "What are your dreams?" "Go for it!"

Those quotes have been a few of the main themes of this book. They were a few of the puzzle pieces that I needed to put together to watch my vision turn into reality. For you to create your reality, you need a place to collect all of your ideas and thoughts. Throughout this book, I will provide you with several places to write down some of your thoughts and dreams. Unfortunately, I didn't give you enough space. When you have time, I suggest that you go out and invest in a journal.

Keep it close by. When that lightning bolt of inspiration hits, pull out your journal and write.

Inspiration comes from hearing a song, reading a quote, seeing a picture, or even hearing a joke. The sad part is, just like lightning, it's gone as quickly as it came. To make that moment last for a lifetime, write about it in your journal.

You never know when you might need a good idea, need to remember a website, or just need that little extra push required to make your dreams come true. By writing down what is in your mind, you can go back and reflect. You can be inspired. You can be motivated. You can remember what you forgot. No matter how you do it, get the ideas out of your head and put them in a form that you can share with yourself and others. This includes a diary, journal, smartphone, notepad, or doodles on a piece of paper. It doesn't matter. Just get the ideas out. This is the first step to achieving your dreams.

Journaling is great. Many of the ideas in this book came from my journal. My wife gave it to me, because I told her about the millions of ideas in my head, and how hard it was to remember them all. I shared my vision, and now you are living my dream.

"Thank you Kelly, I love you!"

Lesson 5

"Stop saying I'll get to it Later."

"You're not finished making a meal until all the dishes are clean."
- My High School Home Economics Teacher

I participated in cooking classes for three years in high school. I heard countless jokes about my last name and participating voluntarily in the classes. I also made a lot of friends on the school bus when I brought my tasty creations home. Things went so well that my teacher suggested that I attend a cooking school after I graduated. Can you imagine a guy named "Kitchen" attending culinary school?

Many of the strategies and techniques I learned in my cooking classes I still use today. Not for cooking, but for life and business. One of the most important lessons taught in the class was to keep our work areas clean. This meant we needed to wash our dishes and cooking utensils as soon as possible. Whether a meal was cooking on the stovetop or baking in the oven, we were taught to clean the dirty cookware while preparing the meal. Our teacher told us this would save us time and make things a lot easier. This was very true. She was teaching us how to be productive with our time. By the time the meal was ready to eat, we didn't have any dishes to clean. Our workspaces were clean and the only things left to clean were the dishes we ate from.

"Fresh from the Kitchen"

I want you to do the following for me right now:

1. Get up from your reading location and take this book you're reading to your kitchen.
2. Survey your kitchen sink.
3. Return to your previous reading location and continue reading.

What did the sink look like? Was it full of dirty dishes? Could you find your silverware hidden under the plates? Were there any pots or pans with the leftover residue from the last meal you cooked? Pretty gross right? Did you see any glasses or bowls with mysterious liquids in them? Yuck! Did you look at all the sink and say, "I don't have time to clean all these dishes.

Life can be the same way. Dirty dishes are the unfinished projects that you started and didn't complete. You need to complete your projects before you start your next one. Unfinished projects build up until they overwhelm you. A pile of dirty dishes is very overwhelming. The way your kitchen sink looks is a reflection of your life. This is the Kitchen Sink Theory.

The dishwasher was invented to relieve you of the burden of washing dishes. When dishes pile up, you put them in the dishwasher and the machine does all the work for you.

"Fresh from the Kitchen"

Unfortunately, life doesn't work the same way. Some people have dishwashers and some don't.

Do you have a dishwasher? In this fast-paced world, everyone is busy. We have limited free time to enjoy life. The same can be said about cooking. Making the meal is fun. Eating the meal is enjoyable. Cleaning up afterward is un-stimulating, but a major part of the process. My cooking classes taught me that it was easier to wash the dishes as I worked. The classes taught me to finish my projects.

Until you clean the dishes in your sink the meal you just made is not complete. You will have a tough time preparing your next culinary masterpiece if the dishes you need are dirty. Letting projects build up eats away at your valuable and limited free time.

The key is to stay on top of things. Don't let one unfinished project after another build-up. If you're letting the dishes in your sink build-up, look at your life. Ask yourself the following questions:

1. Am I letting projects on my to-do list go unfinished or un-started?
2. Am I constantly saying, "I'll get to it later?"

3. Do I wait to begin projects until I have to do them?

4. Do I wait to clean my dishes until I have no dishes to eat from?

If you answered yes to any of these questions, then it's time for you to start cleaning the dishes in your sink. Take the time to clean your dishes as you cook. The five minutes it takes to clean them now is a lot less than twenty minutes it will take you later. Cleaning dishes as you go will make your life easier.

No matter what your next dream project is (writing a book), be sure to tackle it in small manageable amounts. If you wait too long, your dream may appear impossible. Good luck being proactive with your times and staying on top of your dishes! Keep your kitchen clean, because a clean kitchen will inspire you to create the recipes of your dreams.

Lesson 6

"Success Requires Action!"

"Inaction breeds doubt and fear. Action breeds confidence and courage. If you want to conquer fear, do not sit at home and think about it. Go out and get busy." - Dale Carnegie

Any dream you want to live in life is similar to picking apples. You can pick apples from a tree, you can pick them from a display of apples at a market, or you can buy them by the bag at a store. Of course, you can also choose not to get any at all. The thing is that, no matter where you pick your apples, there are different types of right and wrong. Apples can be just right, not ready yet, too ripe, bruised, or rotten.

There are people who pick their own apples, and there are people who have other people pick the apples for them. There are those who just wait for them to fall from the tree. Some don't do anything at all. I want you to be the person who picks their own apples.

"Fresh from the Kitchen"

By picking your own apples, a lot can happen:

1. You will have a great selection to pick from. You can pick one or you can pick many. Some will be just right while others may need time to ripen. You'll also have the ability to avoid the rotten ones. The key is that you will have multiple options!

2. You won't have to worry about someone keeping all the best apples for themselves.

3. You will have a good feeling inside knowing that you made something happen.

4. You will gain knowledge and experiences that I can use for future apple picking.

Success is the achievement of living a dream. Picking apples just like success is hard work. You may have to climb a tree, drag a ladder to the tree, find a cherry picker, knock the tree over, or simply go to the store. You will need help along the way from other apple pickers, too. Your hard work will pay off. You will learn how to take action and be assertive. You will learn how to take advantage of opportunities. You will learn not to wait around for something to happen!

I want to be an apple picker, too! Don't be the person waiting for the apples (your dreams) to fall out of a tree.

“Fresh from the Kitchen”

You never know what you might get. If you pick an apple or two, don’t wait too long to enjoy it. It may begin to rot if you wait too long.

It’s time for me to wrap up this chapter of the book; I’ve got apples to pick. For the other apple pickers in my life, thank you for sharing the knowledge of what to look for, encouraging me to pursue my passions, and showing me how to climb the tree, or where to find a ladder. I plan on picking a lot of apples, and I plan on sharing them with my family, friends, and people I spend time with. Life is short. Pick your apples and don’t let them get old or rotten.

Lesson 7

"Use Your Creativity and Live Your Dreams."

"Creativity is inventing, experimenting, growing, taking risks, breaking rules, making mistakes, and having fun."
- Mary Lou Cook

Everyone participates in activities that require creativity to make them materialize. Dreams don't become reality by following the status quo. Life is short, and there are a ton of activities we want to pursue and experience.

One Spring, I was doing my spring cleaning when I came across an old sketchpad and art supplies. I also found old photos I took for a photography class. Great memories filled my head. Questions populated my head, too. I wondered, "am I as creative as I used to be?"

The answer was yes and no. I remembered the day that I drew a picture at work to welcome people to my office. Most people were surprised that I was the person who drew the picture. They hadn't seen my artistic side. As a child, I would draw all of the time. I turned the visions in my head into reality on paper. Years later, I surprised people by drawing monthly pictures on the information board in my office to make the office more fun.

"Fresh from the Kitchen"

There have been times in my life that I have been creative, and others where I was not. My spring cleaning definitely rekindled my creative juices. I became a kid again.
Kids enjoy almost every aspect of life. They make inanimate objects into toys with their imagination. As adults, our lives can become routine. We neglect opportunities to enjoy the little things. We don't make time to laugh, explore, ask questions, dream, or create.

Spring cleaning helped me discover something: the more I use my creativity, the more I enjoy life. The more I enjoy life, the more productive I am. Life is less boring when you make the most out of every opportunity.

That day I started writing down all of the things that I dreamt of doing. I amazed myself with all the ideas I came up with. I had ideas for the people close to me and for myself. As a professional speaker and coach, I'm responsible for assisting leaders with living their dreams. They ask me to use my creativity to aid them, but why wasn't I doing the same for myself?

I decided to take my own advice: life isn't all about your work. You need to pursue activities you are truly passionate about. As people, we need to be creative with everything we do. I encourage you to make time to rediscover your past so you can truly appreciate the present and create the future you desire.

Lesson 8

"Stop making New Year's Resolutions."

"Set a goal and follow through. The world is full of unachieved yet reachable goals! Never give up!" - Unknown

At the end of every year, people around the world make New Year's resolutions. Essentially they wait all year to get started on something they consider important. I researched the definition of resolution online. Here's what Google said:

Resolution: (noun) - A firm decision to do or not do something.

(noun) - the quality of being determined or resolute.

I don't know about you, but those definitions sound a lot like the definition for goals.

Goals: (noun) the object of a person's ambition or effort; an aim or desired result.

Call it a semantics thing, but I like to make Goals. When you make a goal, you start to consider the plan needed to make it a reality.

"Fresh from the Kitchen"

Napoleon Hill wrote, "A goal is a dream with a deadline." You must take action to make your dreams a reality. You need a plan with action steps.

Action Steps: (verb) a measure or action, especially one of a series taken in order to deal with or achieve a particular thing.

New Year's Eve is a time of excitement. People around the world celebrate the beginning of a New Year. The New Year provides a clean slate. It's a time to devise resolutions that will produce an extraordinary year.

Every New Year's Eve, I'm presented with the same question: "what are your resolutions for the New Year?" My answer always results in dumbfounded looks: "I don't make resolutions!" I tell them that I make goals with action steps. People give me a confused look, and ask me what the difference is.

Look at the definition above. A resolution is the decision to do something. There isn't any action there. Making a goal means your ambitions and desires are one step closer to becoming reality. Goals can be measured. Goals need to be written down. The next course of action is to write down the steps needed to achieve your goals. The goals and action steps have to be measurable.

"Fresh from the Kitchen"

How many people have you heard say, "I want to lose weight in the New Year." This is their New Year's resolution. They never state how much weight they want to lose or give a deadline for losing the weight.

Goals have measurable objectives, a timeline, and actions steps.

Here is an example: an individual weighs 200 pounds. They make a resolution to lose weight in the New Year. At the end of the year, they weigh 199 pounds. They have successfully accomplished their resolution, but are disappointed because they wanted to weigh 175 pounds. They made a resolution, not a goal. With a clearly defined objective and action plan, the chances of achieving a goal increase immensely.

There's nothing wrong with making a resolution, but people say a lot of things they never do. I talk a lot, and dream a lot too. The way I challenge myself to achieve my dreams is to create a plan. To take this a step further, I send my goals and action steps to my closest friends. My success team is there to offer support, knowledge, experience, and friendship. They are there to kick my butt when I slack off, too!

I wish everyone the best of luck as you achieve your resolutions and goals. The best time to start living any goal is right now. Any day can be your "New Year." Remember this: goal setting is like grocery shopping. You can say that you need to go shopping, but if you don't make a list, you always end up forgetting something important.

Lesson 9

"Have a Grocery List of Dreams You Hunger For."

"It must be borne in mind that the tragedy of life doesn't lie in not reaching your goal. The tragedy lies in having no goal to reach."
- Benjamin E. Mays

Life is all about wants and needs. There are many things we need and even more things we want. In short, life is like a menu at your favourite restaurant. When you go, you will see many things that you want and several you hunger for. People are very visual. Without a detailed list, you can become distracted easily. I call distractions "Shiny Objects." These objects appear to be fun and exciting, but steal away valuable time and resources you should commit your important wants and needs.

Stores are designed to appeal to your visual stimuli. Many of these stimuli are on your grocery list. Most are not on your list. They appeal to your impulsive side. As you shop, you determine what fits into your current budget and schedule. The important factor is to have the items on a list so you don't forget them. If you don't get them this week, you'll get them in the future.

People who don't shop with a list end up buying what they don't need, what they don't want, or something they have too many of. Does this sound like your life?

"Fresh from the Kitchen"

Many of us don't have a "life grocery list." This is a list of dreams. What do you need and want to do with your life? It is amazing to see what you really want and need out of life when you write it down. My challenge to you is to take a couple of sheets of paper and a couple of hours alone to write or draw everything you want and need in life. There is no limit to what you write. This is a list of things you can work to achieve for the rest of your life.

Please email me at FRESH@FRANKKITCHEN.COM for a free PDF of my Grocery List worksheet.

There will be people who complete their lists faster than others. Just remember: this is your grocery list. You can always add items to the list as you think about them. As you complete an item on your list, cross it out and write the date you lived your dream. As you start to cross items out, you will experience the feeling of accomplishment. You may not be able to cross many of the items off the list now, but you can always go back to the list to remember what you wrote down. Without a dream, there are no goals!

Do remember the old statement: "out of sight, out of mind." Writing down your dreams is the first step to achieving them and living them. Reviewing your dreams during the year will inspire you to complete the ones you haven't crossed off your list.

"Your future hasn't been written yet. No one has. Your future is whatever you make it. So make it a good one."

- Doc Brown – Back to the Future 3

"Fresh from the Kitchen"

No matter your age, it is never too early, or too late, to make a grocery list. You can always add more to your grocery list. It is never too late to add items to your grocery list. Grab a piece of paper and get started. Go ahead, start now, before you read the next chapter. I've included a few items on my grocery list that I haven't lived yet to provide you with a little inspiration.

Frank Kitchen's Grocery List:

(As of January 1, 2020)

I will take Kelly on a vacation to celebrate our 10th wedding Anniversary

I will be debt free by age 48 (9/4/2021)

I will write and publish a children's book

I will attend an Olympic games with my family

I will be a travel show host

I will own a home

I will visit my birthplace in Germany

I will speak professional in all 50 states

I will be the commencement speaker at Lakeland CC

I will generate $1million in speaking earnings by age 50

Lesson 10

"Have a Plan…to Live Your Dreams."

"A dream without a goal is a wish. A goal without a plan is just a dream" – Unknown

Have you ever watched a political debate? The politicians offer advice and tell people what needs to be done. It's tough to believe in politicians when you find out they are doing the opposite of what they preach. If you take a minute to reflect, many of the politicians sound just like us.

During the United States Presidential election of 2008, I began to think about the comments that I make to people. We often hear the political candidates go back and forth about their dreams for the community. We hear about what they will do when they get into office. The candidates all have dreams.

Dreams are nice, but people want to know: is there a plan? Yes, we can go to a political website to learn more, but people want to hear more of what you are going to do versus what you would like to do.

As humorous as this may sound, we are just like the people running for political office. We talk about our dreams. We talk about what we would do if "x" happens. But just like the candidates and politicians, we don't talk about our plans.

"Fresh from the Kitchen"

Dreams are defined the following ways:

1. A series of thoughts, images and sensations occurring in a person's mind.
2. A cherished aspiration, ambition or ideal.
3. An unrealistic or self-deluding fantasy.

People want reality, not dreams. Do you waste a lot of time and energy just dreaming? Are you focused on the wrong thing? Do you get distracted easily? Dreaming is a wonderful thing. A world without dreamers would be a boring place. The key is to use some of your valuable time and energy to plan it out after you dream it. Dreams do not magically come true. Plans and actions make dreams come true. You have to make your dreams turn into reality.

I'm sure that you are thinking, *dreams are fun and plans are boring!* Yes, it's true that plans are no fun. Experiencing a dream come true is a lot of fun. Remember, all successful people have a plan to make their dreams become reality. They share their dreams and plans with supportive people. You can call them boring, but they are having fun. They are enjoying life while dreamers are simply dreaming about having fun.

Good luck as you turn your dreams into reality. It's nice to talk about dreams, but it is more fun to see them become reality. I'll end this chapter with a classic line from a television show from the 1980s: *"I love it when a plan comes together!" – The A-Team*

Lesson 11

"Have a Personal Mission Statement."

"Without a mission statement, you may get to the top of the ladder and then realize it was leaning against the wrong building."
- Dave Ramsey

I'm invited to speak at conferences and workshops worldwide. I'll admit that it's a cool career. I get to give organizations and businesses advice on how to improve themselves both personally and professionally. I speak about setting goals and discovering your purpose. The people that I work with constantly provide me with great feedback, comments, and ideas.

Their comments cause me to think: I am a goal-oriented person. I always set goals for myself, but I wasn't setting my goals with a main purpose in mind. Life is a marathon, but I'd been training for short races. I decided to make a personal mission statement for myself. I needed to set a goal for the race called life.

Here's what I came up with. It's my mission statement with objectives on how to accomplish my mission.

The Mission Statement of Frank Cornelius Kitchen (2012)

The mission for Frank Cornelius Kitchen is to live a life full of positive experiences. My mission will be achieved by doing the following

1. Sharing my dreams, goals, feelings, and thoughts with people close to me.
2. Dealing with others with honesty, integrity, tolerance, compassion and respect.
3. Sharing, teaching and coaching what I've learned.
4. Having a positive influence on the people that I come in contact with.
5. Making life fun and enjoyable.
6. Practicing what I preach.
7. Displaying financial and fiscal responsibility.
8. Capitalizing on opportunities to learn, improve and educate myself.
9. Taking care of myself physically.
10. Putting myself in positive and productive environments.
11. Traveling as much as possible.
12. Being open, and respectful to new ideas and experiences.

I've shared my mission statement with you; what is your mission statement and whom will you share it with? Get started now on by writing your mission statement on a piece of paper and display it for all to see.

Lesson 12

"Build a Winning Team to Support You and Your Dreams!"

"What is not started today is never finished tomorrow."
- Johann Wolfgang von Goethe

I'm definitely a goal-oriented person. I like having something written down to hold me accountable. A specific target to shoot for. You can call it a resolution, goal, oath, promise, decree, declaration, or pledge, but you need to write it down. Put it somewhere visible. And most importantly, you must share the information with the people closest to you. People who are willing to challenge you and hold you accountable.

One summer, I started meeting with a good friend, Kyle Graham. We met to share our personal and professional goals. We also shared information to help us achieve our goals. Every time we met, the pressure was on to prove we were working on our goals. When Kyle and his wife moved away, we kept in touch through email. I wrote to check on him and he thanked me for reminding him about his goals.

One morning, I opened an email from Kyle. He asked me how I was doing with my goals. I thanked him for the small push. I set many goals that summer and I'm proud to say I met or surpassed most of them. I didn't recognize this until I wrote him to give him my progress report.

While typing my report, I started to think about that year. I always planned for the year to be a better year than my previous one. I realized that it's hard to achieve your goals if you don't share them with the people who are close to you.

I read a book titled *Get off your Butt and Do it Now* by friend and mentor, Jermaine M. Davis. In the book he talks about developing a team to support you. Goals are dreams with plans and a deadline. Your support team makes it possible for your dreams to come true. Your support group should consist of people you trust, people who will push and support you during your endeavors. I have developed a strong team over the years. By sharing my goals, I had double pressure. If I don't pursue my goals, I will be letting myself down, but I will also let my team down. I truly believe that you cannot reach your goals if you keep them inside. There's research to back my option too. When you're proud of something, you have to share it with other people. This can be verbal or visual; the key is to share.

When you are thinking about your next set of New Year's resolutions, be sure to think about the people you will share your resolution with. Create a name for them and let them know you're asking for their assistance with your resolutions. Type or write out your resolutions and put them somewhere you can see them. Give that list to your team and ask them to remind you or help you with your resolutions.

Who knows, they may ask you to do the same thing for them. It's amazing what you can achieve when you have constant reminders. Remember: "out of sight, out of mind." Good luck to everyone! Think positive, and turn those resolutions into reality.

Are you ready to create your *support team*? The time is now. Please use a separate piece of paper or a journal to put your team together. Write down their name, birthday, address, email, phone number, and why you want them on your team. These people will assist you in making your dreams come true. After you add them to your list. Please contact them to let them know why you want them as a part of your team. Your entry(ies) should look like this:

______________________________'s Support Team

Name:
Birthday:
Address:

E-mail:
Phone Number:
What makes them special?

Lesson 13

"Read Often and Apply What You Learned."

"Poetry is when an emotion has found its thought and the thought has found words." - Robert Frost

People ask me a lot of questions. They ask me for advice. They ask me about my life. They ask me for recommendations. One of the most common questions is, "What books would you recommend for reading?" It's an interesting question considering I grew up in the television generation.

I didn't become an avid reader until recently. I read an article about the habits of the most successful people in the world. One of the most common habits was reading! They read and they read often. Blinklist Magazine reported in 2018 that Warren Buffet spends 80% of his day reading. The Huffington Post reported that 2016 that Bill Gates reads 50 non-fiction books every year.

Billionaires, CEO, Leaders, and people of influence all read. Inc. Magazine shared in 2017 that, "Most CEOs and executives read 4-5 books per month." This is about 45 minutes a day! These people are reading everything possible (trade journals, articles, websites, blogs, etc) to fill their brains with that knowledge that helps them grow personally and professionally.

"Fresh from the Kitchen"

In 2019, I set a goal to dedicate more time to reading. My goal, one book per month. A goal I blew away. I read books and listened to audiobooks while driving and working out. Guess what happened? I had my most productive and profitable business year ever. My excuse of not having enough time to read was proven wrong. The knowledge I gained was applied and produced noticeable results. So, what are you feeding your mind? Are you feeding it information to help you grow?

Here are a few books that have helped me live my dreams:

1. The Bible
2. "Book More Business" by Lois Creamer
3. "The Dream Manager" by Matthew Kelly
4. "Think and Grow Rich" by Napoleon Hill
5. "Caught between a Dream and a Job" by Delatorro McNeal
6. "Get off your Butt and Do it Now." by Dr. Jermaine M. Davis
7. "168 Hours" by Laura Vauderkam
8. "You are a Badass" by Jen Sincero
9. "Value-Based Fees" by Alan Weiss
10. "Becoming" by Michelle Obama
11. "The Virgin Way" by Richard Branson
12. "Eat That Frog!" by Brian Tracy
13. "Quiet Strength"by Tony Dungy
14. "The China Study" by T. Colin Campbell, Ph.D.

Lesson 14

"Build A Soundtrack for Success."

"Play some good tunes." – Anthony Marino

In my 20s, Friday nights were the nights I went out with my friends. Most Fridays were spent with my friend Tony. It didn't matter what we did as long as we were together. No matter who drove, I knew what Tony would say, "play some good tunes kid." Tony loved music. The music that we played in the car put us in a good mood. The better the music, the better the experience.

"Listening to music can decrease your stress hormones by 20%." - Livestrong.com

Music has to be one of the most influential creations of mankind. No matter the genre, music has the amazing ability to spark memories, emotions, and behaviors. People spend a lot of time watching television. In 2019, *The United States Bureau of Labor Statistics* reported that the people will spend over 15 years of their life watching television or viewing social media.

My question is how much of this media do people really remember?

Music brings back memories of a specific date or time instantly. While writing this book, I listened to music.

"Fresh from the Kitchen"

During a recent move, I discovered a box full of CDs that Tony made for me. Every weekend, he would use his computer to put together a new *Marino Mix CD* to get us energized before we went out for the night. One of his favorite CDs to play was the soundtrack from the *Rocky* movies. I decided to play one of Tony's CDs and good memories filled my head. It was as if I were listening to the soundtrack of my twenties. I started to remember funny moments. I could remember exactly where I first heard a song. In many cases, I could remember who I was with when the song played. Music is incredible.

Do you listen to music? What do you listen to? My musical taste varies. I have learned to pay attention to the lyrics and instruments. The talent that it takes to master an instrument is remarkable. Song lyrics contain words that can inspire and motivate. I've watched my kids' moods change simply by the tone of a song.

Music can be the catalyst for positive experiences. Charles F. Emory of *The Ohio State University* reported that music increases a person's ability to organize cognitive output. No matter the music played during his study, participants reported feeling better emotionally and mentally after working out with music, versus no music.

"Fresh from the Kitchen"

I'm not a scientist, but I have seen the positive results of implementing music into my personal and professional life. I know that music makes me more productive. I work more efficiently when I have music on. Music gives me ideas when I'm brainstorming ideas for speeches. Music puts me in the right mood before I go onstage. Music adds so much to our lives. It can provide the theme for a high school dance. Music is used to set the mood and tone of movies. It gets people's attention when played at the beginning of a wedding. It is played at important events and ceremonies. Simply put, music is the soundtrack of our lives.

I want you to be as productive as possible. The best way to do this is to compile a personal soundtrack. If your life were a movie and it had a soundtrack, what songs would you choose?

On a piece of paper, write down up to sixteen song titles with the artist's name. This is your personal soundtrack. This soundtrack will consist of the songs that inspire and motivate you to be your best, to never quit, and do the unthinkable. Save this soundtrack on whatever device you listen to music with. Can you hear the songs in your head right now? Do you feel that smile on your face? Can you sense the energy filling your body? This is what music does to us. It is the feeling of listening to good tunes kid.

"Fresh from the Kitchen"

Your list should look like this:

________________________________'s Soundtrack

Song Title and Artist

1.
2.
3.
4.
5.
6.
7.
8.
9.
10.
11.
12.
13.
14.
15.
16.

Lesson 15

"Don't let Obstacles Stop You or Your Dreams."

"Giving that extra degree makes all the difference."
- Drew Brees, NFL Quarterback

There are moments in our lives where we become inspired to achieve, attempt, or pursue an aspiration, to hope or dream. Movies can inspire us, people can inspire us, books can inspire us, and various forms of social media can inspire us. I am inspired by great conversations with co-workers, students, friends, and family. Conversations can be very motivating.

I love to hear stories of people achieving the impossible. When I hear these stories, it makes me think of all the things I can do. Here is the amazing story of my friend and former student Katie Spotz.

Attending a college or university can cost an unthinkable amount of money. The price tag can strike fear in a lot of people. The total cost can cause prospective students to give up on their dream of obtaining a college education. There are many ways to find the money to pay for a college degree, but most people don't know where to look. They don't believe that there is money available. They don't do the research, or ask the proper questions. Many just quit and join the workforce.

"Fresh from the Kitchen"

Courageous individuals look in the mirror and take action. They lead and motivate themselves toward achieving their dreams. Their determination keeps their enthusiasm alive.

My friend Katie faced this very situation when it came time to attend college. She had good grades, but her family didn't have the money to pay for the school she wanted to attend. She discussed her dream of getting her college degree with several friends. They suggested she apply for scholarships and grants. She didn't know much about the pots of free money available to prospective college students.

She began to ask questions of people with knowledge on the subject. The answers that she received excited her. She began to spend her free time researching grants and scholarships. She discovered that she would have to fill out long applications, write longer essays, collect letters of recommendation, and in some cases, be interviewed face to face. All these barriers make most people quit, but not Katie. She was determined to find the money to pay for her education.

Katie endured many failures. She applied for over thirty different grants and scholarships. Many organizations she applied to never responded. That just made her more determined to apply for more scholarships. Each time she applied, she needed more letters of recommendation. I was one of the letter writers, so I quickly became invested in her dream. Many of the organizations she applied to, I had never heard of.

More than two-thirds declined her applications. Many would consider this a failure, but Katie was happy.

Several of the grants and scholarships were approved. None of them were for huge amounts of money, but when they were all added together, I was amazed when I found out her entire education was paid for.

This experience only increased Katie's confidence. She has pursued amazing opportunities. As I write, her list of achievements continues to grow. She is a member of the United States Coast Guard. She has participated in educational programs and community service projects in North Carolina, California, Australia, New Zealand, and Thailand. She received her college degree. She completed a three thousand mile bike ride to raise money for the *American Lung Association.* She even rowed a boat solo across the Atlantic Ocean to raise money for the *Blue Planet Run Foundation*. It is amazing what Katie's determination has done. All this started when Katie put in the extra effort to chase her dreams of obtaining a college education. I'll bet that you and I both would be equally amazed at what our determination can produce.

For more information on Katie and her amazing adventures, please look her up on the internet or visit her website:

www.katiespotz.com

Lesson 16

"Get Comfortable being Uncomfortable."

"You need to be comfortable being uncomfortable."
- Dr. Bernard Franklin

I truly didn't understand the quote Dr. Bernard Franklin shared with me until one fateful day. I'm always told how well I relate to new people and situations. I put those comments to the test when I visited a local meeting of *Rotary International.*

I wanted to learn more about the organization. I also wanted to introduce myself to the organization's leadership and members. Rotary was about to send me and four other professionals to Australia as a part of their Group Study Exchange Program (GSE). I was asked to spend four weeks in a foreign country as an ambassador and representative of Northeast Ohio. Meeting the people I would be representing was a logical decision.

When I arrived for the meeting, I introduced myself to their President. The next thing I knew, I was on the agenda speaking to a room full of local business and civic leaders. My heart was beating a million times an hour. **(This was before I became a professional speaker)**

Once I got to the front of the room, and was handed the microphone, things changed. I smile when I think about how I was truly comfortable in an uncomfortable situation.

I was comfortable because I took Dr. Franklin's advice. I saw this as a new challenge and great preparation for my trip to Australia. Before I knew it, my time was done. I had spoken to a room full of strangers. I had fully explained who I was, why I was there, what the trip was about, and answered questions. After the meeting, several people came up to congratulate me and tell me how well I had spoken in front of a group. They invited me to come back and speak again. I was also invited to speak for other organizations.

A few minutes before things started, I was nervous and had no clue what I was going to say; I took a deep breath and the rest is history. It is important that you never let them see you sweat. I took an uncomfortable situation and made it into a comfortable one. This was the beginning of my speaking career.

That day was a great experience. It was also a great example of what I was taught years before: "be comfortable being uncomfortable." We are always going to experience new nerve-racking situations. You need to take every new situation as a personal challenge. You must tackle new situations and build upon them. Your new experiences become past experiences that you have learned from. Every new experience in your life is an opportunity for growth. I confidently know that I can now go into a room full of strangers and perform on the spot.

"Fresh from the Kitchen"

Life is about experiences. More than a few will be uncomfortable, but you'll have some great stories to share once you tackle them.

To learn more about Rotary International and the Group Study Exchange program, go to: **www.Rotary.org**.

Lesson 17

"Have the Courage to Pursue Your Dreams."

"Better to Face Danger than to Always be in Fear."
– Chinese Proverb

Courage is defined as the ability or strength possessed to do something that frightens us. People fear the unknown. It makes them uncomfortable. People face situations that frighten them daily; trying a new food item on the menu, moving away from family and friends, getting a gym membership, stepping out onto a dance floor, speaking in public, or asking questions. Fear can prevent people from having the opportunity to gain knowledge, have new experiences and live their dream.s

Confidence in a person, situation, or dream comes from knowledge and experience. The youth of the world have many experiences where they display courage. There is a magical age when most teenagers display a lot of courage and don't recognize it. That age is 16. At 16, most teenagers are given the right to obtain a vehicle operator's license from their local Department of Motor Vehicles.

"Fresh from the Kitchen"

This moment brings about frightful thoughts in the minds of parents worldwide. "Can we afford a car?" "How much will insurance be?" "Do we trust ________ with our car?" "What if ______ gets into an accident?" "There are a lot of dangerous drivers on the road!"

"Have you seen _______ drive at the go-kart track?" These are just a few of the thoughts expressed or not expressed by parents.

While parents are freaking out, teenagers are imagining all of the possibilities. "I don't have to ride my bike." "My car will be just like the celebrities on Youtube!" "I'm going to drive my friends everywhere!" "Mom and Dad don't have to take me to parties." "No more school bus!" "Road Trip!"

Children are fearless. This is the greatest time of growth. Children are often referred to as sponges. Children crave the knowledge necessary to make their dreams come true. They seem to ask millions of questions. If a child wants to know how something works, they will approach a stranger to ask questions: "why?" or "how?"

Parents actually teach their children to ask questions. Then, we start to grow up and fear the answers we may get. Many times, we don't ask questions because we fear the unknown. Instead of fearing the unknown, a leader embraces the possibilities of the future, just like the new driver.

The new driver can fear all of the negatives of accepting the role of motor vehicle operator, or embrace all of the possibilities.

You will see many teenagers get into a "heated discussion" with their parents about how they will avoid all of the things that can go wrong. This is what a leader does. They don't fear all of the negatives and the unknown. They imagine all of the positives that can occur. At this point, they begin to grow.

They gain new experiences that they would never have experienced if they had allowed fear to hold them back. It is okay to acknowledge the fear, but also to think of all of the possibilities.

The next time you need the courage to take action, reflect on your youth. You weren't perfect the first time that you drove a car. You were nervous, and a little fearful, of what could happen. Your parents' comments made you fear the unknown. Eventually, you began driving and, every day, you gained a little more confidence. The more you drove your car, the more courage you gained. Life is the same way. You look forward to all of the new experiences. Every new experience gets you closer to living your dreams. Every new experience increases your confidence and gives you the courage to pursue possibilities.

Lesson 18

"A Negative Mindset Leads to Negative Results."

"Life can be one big traffic jam. You can stay stuck on the highway of life or you can find a way around the traffic."
– Frank Kitchen

Why is it that every time you have to be somewhere at a specific time, you seem to run into traffic? There are unexpected car accidents, slow drivers, household appliances in the middle of the road, unnecessary construction, and roadblocks. I've learned that possessing a negative attitude, showcasing negative actions, or making negative comments are all mental roadblocks.

When a roadblock appears, detours must be found. Questions must be asked: "What now?" "What can I do?" and "What are the possibilities?" Navigating around any roadblock takes action. Mostly, it's hard work, especially when you don't have GPS or your cell phone. There are people who feel it is easier to stay in one spot and complain, but complaining and being negative gets you nowhere. Have you seen people do this? Have you ever sat in one place and complained about not advancing. Isn't that more frustrating than the hard work of navigating around the roadblock?

Last Lecture author Randy Pausch said that "barriers are put into our lives for the purpose of showing how badly we want something." Negativity is a huge barrier for a lot of people. It's easy to be negative. When someone asks, "tell me something good about yourself," it takes time, it requires thought.

When you're asked to think about the negative, the answers come easy. Why is that? Our world constantly bombards us with negative messaging. People invariably say, "that's just the way it is!" But I ask, "does it have to be that way?" and "what can be done to change the situation?" Positive people will come up with a list of options and plans to improve their situation. Negative people will complain about all the reasons things can't work. Both require the same amount of energy but produce vastly different results.

Negative people bring the people down. Positive people inspire and empower people. Ultimately, it's up to the negative people to look at themselves in the mirror and mentally challenge themselves to change their mindset. It takes work, but eventually they discover that it is more productive to be positive than it is to give up when they encounter a roadblock. Being negative is the mental roadblock to people advancing in life. When you choose your mindset you're choosing the results you can cook up.

Lesson 19

"You are a Leader!"

"Where there is no vision, the people will perish."
– Proverbs 29:18

"Share the vision, live the dream" is one of my favorite quotes. The man who said it wrote the forward to this book. His name is Rodger Campbell. He is one of the many people who inspired me to write this book. His quote inspires people worldwide to be leaders. Leaders are individuals who educate, elevate, empower themselves and others to live a dream.

A dream is a cherished aspiration, ambition, or ideal. There are different names for dreams. People call them visions, goals, objectives, ideas, plans, targets, or fantasies. No matter the name, we all have them. Individuals and organizations are inspired by dreams. Countless dreams have become reality. It takes just one person to get the ball rolling...a leader!

I have a former student and friend named Oloho Delano (O-Lo-Ho). He felt strongly about the events of September 11, 2001. He was so moved by the events that he traveled to New York City shortly after the tragedy to see what he and a small group from his church could do.

As the one-year anniversary of the event approached, he felt that our college should sponsor an event to honor the people who lost their lives on that day. He discovered that the college was having a small ceremony the morning of September 11, 2002. There would be a moment of silence; there would be brief words of remembrance, and the school flags would be lowered to half-mast. My student felt more should be done. He wanted the school to do more. His passionate convictions motivated him to action.

Oloho came to my office to talk about his dream for a Remembrance Program and a day full of community building activities. He wanted to know what he could do to make his dream possible. Oh, the questions he had. He described what he wanted to do in such detail that I could visualize the day in my mind. I was truly inspired. At that moment, we put together a list of everyone necessary to make his dream come true. We crafted a proposal to present to several departments and community organizations. Oloho displayed the same passion he had in my office to everyone he came in contact with. Before I knew it, he had organized a group of students and volunteers, reserved a venue, constructed a marketing plan, and recruited a Master of Ceremonies – me.

When September 11, 2002 arrived, the day began with the school holding its morning ceremony. After the ceremony, Oloho's events began. He made arrangements to have a memorial plaque and two twin evergreen trees dedicated on school property.

He designed the plaque and picked out the stone that it was mounted to. It honored the lives of the people lost on that terrible day. The trees represented the beginning of life versus the end of it. During the day, he gave away tree saplings to anyone who wanted them.

The theme of the day was to honor life, not to take it. The rest of the day consisted of Oloho and his volunteers informing classes and the community of that night's program.

Oloho was nervous when the program began, but he didn't need to be. The singers, dancers, and speakers performed to a packed house at the college's theater. He even recited a self-written poem that brought tears to the eyes of the people in the audience. When the night ended, people thanked the students for the day's activities. Many of the people discussed how professional and well-run the day's events were. They were amazed when they discovered the person responsible was a student. Leadership is about action not tiles. Leaders are remembered more for their actions more than their words. Oloho shared his vision and we all lived his dream. How exciting is that?

Lesson 20

"Leadership is an Action not a Title."

"I never dreamed about success. I worked for it." -Estee Lauder

Leadership isn't easy. It requires time, energy, and both physical and fiscal investments. As I stated in the last chapter, I believe you are a leader and *leadership* is the ability to educate, elevate, and empower an individual or group to live a dream. We all want to be successful leaders, and we want to work with positive and productive leaders. The dilemma with leadership is that we focus so much on the dream or outcome that we forget about the little things that will make us a leader who is remembered for producing positive results. Results that inspire others.

Being a leader requires a little luck. The ultimate lucky number is *seven*. Here are *Seven Little Things* that you can do to develop a highly productive leadership style that produces results. Remember the toughest person you'll ever lead is yourself.

I've been blessed to work with, meet and study the leadership styles of some amazing leaders. The most productive displayed these actions. Actions I work replicate daily.

1. Show Genuine Interest in the people you lead

Study the people you lead, including yourself. Know their strengths and their opportunities for growth; know their likes and dislikes, know their motivations. Don't treat the people you lead like a number. Know each person as an individual. Make them feel special.

2. Be Visible

Be a role model. Set the example. Show up for the activities you ask others to attend. Let people see you working. Actively display the behaviors you want people to exhibit.

3. Be a Teacher

Provide people with a vision and teach people how to make that vision come true. Invest the time and resources to train people thoroughly and constantly. Develop a training program that helps people grow.

4. Delegate

You can't do everything yourself. Discover the talents of the people you lead. Use their talents to accomplish the goal or vision. Put people in positions to excel and grow.

5. Do the S-ugar H-oney I-ce T-ea Jobs!

Don't delegate only dirty jobs to people. Show everyone that you are willing to get dirty, too. When people see you doing the tough jobs, you will earn their respect.

6. Be Consistent.

Consistent Communication, Consistent Actions, Consistent Work and Honesty are the keys to success. Truthfully explain why decisions are made. A lack of consistency in the way you treat and communicate with others can lead to rumors, uncertainty, and distrust. Be fair and keep things professional versus personal.

7. Reward People

We are quick to criticize people, but slow to recognize people. All feedback must be given at the proper time. This is especially true for positive feedback or rewards. Some people require a simple *thank you.* Other people require more. Find ways to celebrate every accomplishment or visual display of growth. If you truly know the people you lead, finding unique ways to reward them won't be a problem.

Lesson 21

"Embrace what Makes You Unique."

"It takes more courage to reveal insecurities than to hide them."
- Alex Karras

The letters FCK make up my initials. My name is Frank Cornelius Kitchen. Yes, I am named after a room in a house. My name has provided me with a lifetime of teasing, questions, and strength. People have asked, "do you cook franks in the kitchen?" I've been referred to as living room, dining room, bathroom, and bedroom. It took me years to learn how to spell my middle name. When I got older, I learned my initials are not the best initials when I have to initial important documents. I tell everyone that it could have been worse. My parents could have named me Frank Ulysses Kitchen. I'll give you time to figure out those initials.

My name could have caused a lot of mental scars, but my name has given me strength. I often tell audiences how my mom loved monogramming everything she purchased for me as a child. I had interesting discussions with my high school teachers when I showed up to school wearing a monogrammed turtleneck and backpack. They were monogrammed with the letters FCK.

"Fresh from the Kitchen"

There are people who consider my name a joke. For me, the joke has turned into a source of pride and strength. My mom informed me that she gave me my name to let me know who I am, where I come from and who I can be. I am a **F-**undraiser, **C**-oach, and **K**-eynote Speaker. I am named after my father and grandfather. My first name is my father's name and my middle name is my grandfather's name. Both have served the United States in the armed forces. They have protected the freedoms that I enjoy today. They have provided me the freedom to write this book. I also have one of the most memorable last names. No one ever forgets the guy named *Kitchen.* You also find the work FRESH in the 21 letters that make up my name. **Fr**ank Corn**e**liu**s** Kitc**h**en. My mom really knew what she was doing.

My initials are interesting and unique. I was taught that you need a *hook* when it comes to marketing yourself. My initials have become that hook for me and my business. I've made t-shirts using them. How amazing is it to have the pastor of your church ask for a t-shirt that reads *FCK* on the front and *All I need is U* on the back? I tell people around the world that, "I provide *Fresh* and *Creative Knowledge* that educates, elevates and empowers leaders around the world to be the positive difference makers and life changers needed in their organizations and communities; to do this, all I need is "U" and an opportunity to shine."
Life should be enjoyed. You should have fun. No one is perfect. You possess unique abilities and talents. They can hold you back or give you strength. The choice is yours.

Lesson 22

"Everyone needs a Role Model, Mentor or Coach."

"We learn 80% of what we need by the age of four years old, the rest of our life is spent perfecting what we have learned."

- Edith Mack Gordon

Do you remember when you were a child? Do you remember your lack of fear? Do you remember the constant energy that you had? Do you remember your constant quest to discover how everything works? Can you believe the hairstyles and clothes your parents forced on you? Do you ever wish you could go back and do it all over again?

When I was growing up, everyone knew me as Frankie. My dad was Frank, so I was called Frankie. There is a picture of Frankie on the back cover of this book. He's there because he is one of my role models. Frankie was a cool kid. His afro was remarkable. His smile lit up a room. His questions were constant. He was an explorer. He had a solution for every problem. He loved to play sports. He was inventive. He got along with everyone. He was a dreamer.

"Fresh from the Kitchen"

One of Frankie's dreams was to be older and taller, so everyone would stop treating him like a child. He told everyone to call him Frank when he turned 13. At 13, he was no longer a child. He was a teenager. "Teenagers don't have kid nicknames" was his proclamation.

He didn't want to be treated like a child anymore. No more sitting at the kid's table for family holidays. No babysitters. No bedtime. This was laughable considering he still played with his Voltron and GI Joe toys. He would go Trick or Treating, had no facial hair on his face, was shorter than all of the girls in school, and spent time at home making the world's best lemon cakes in his sister's Easy Bake Oven.

I miss Frankie. As I've aged, I've become Frank to everyone. A few people still call me Frankie, mostly family and friends who have known me for a long time. Every time I hear that name, a smile comes to my face. I spent my childhood wanting to be an adult; now, I spend my adult years wishing I could be that little kid again.

As we grow older, society tells us to stop acting like a child. We are told to be serious, and to grow up. We grow up and forget about what makes life fun and interesting. Getting older doesn't mean we can't have fun in our lives. Instead of thinking why or why not, adults start thinking no or that's not possible.

"Fresh from the Kitchen"

Children should be our role models. They are sponges. They learn anything and everything at an amazing rate. They apply what they learn instantly. To a child, everything is possible. Discovery is a fun challenge. There's always a back door or another way. They enjoy the challenge of getting things done. The simplest things can be turned into something fun and exciting.

When I watch my kids play, I often think, I would love to be five years old again - minus the afro and polyester suit. I would love to have the passion and spirit to appreciate the little things. I want to explore the world, laugh all the time, spend time with friends, do things I enjoy and not worry about what other people think; I want to enjoy life.

The reality is, I can still be that kid. You can too. Everyday my kids teach me what we can all do. We can explore and live life to the fullest. We can replicate the actions of people we consider our role models. We can ask a person we admire to mentor us. We can seek out a coach to assist us with living our personal or professional dreams.

Who are your role models?

1.

2.

3.

4.

What traits does your Role Model possess that you would like to replicate?

1.

2.

3.

4.

Are you willing to seek out and invest in a mentorship or coaching program to improve your opportunities of living your dreams? Contact them as soon as possible!

Lesson 23

"Do it Mentally before You do it Physically."

"Dress for the job you want, not the job you have!"
– Unknown

I really like the quote above. My best friend Scott Cummings shared it with me while we were on vacation. The quote came up while we were sitting by the pool at a Las Vegas hotel. We were talking about people pursuing their dreams. We were discussing why people succeed or fail in achieving their dreams.

I believe the quote is all about an individual's mindset. Everyone has dreams, but what are you doing mentally to achieve your dreams? Before you can physically do something, you have to imagine it. You have to completely believe that you can do it mentally. You must be able to speak it aloud with confidence and excitement.

I read an article about actor Matthew McConaughey that weekend. He was quoted several times in the article. One particular quote opened my eyes. He said, "you have to tie your shoes first." He was talking about running. Simply put, he was saying that you have to prepare mentally for the activity you are going to do *before* you do it.

My friend Dr. Brian Hester shared with me over tea how he educates his clients that the best time to start something, is to commit to it now.

Many people think they can turn a switch and change overnight. Here are a few examples.

Example #1
A smoker talks about how he wants to quit smoking. In order to dress the part, he needs to start cutting back on his smoking. He has to start mentally acting like a non-smoker.

Example #2
People go on fad diets or have surgery to help them lose weight. Months later, the weight is back on. Mentally, they never changed the habits that created their health issues. They didn't commit to a healthy lifestyle or exercise routine.

Example #3
People talk about taking care of their finances. They talk about what they're going to do when they get out of debt. Talk is great, but what are they doing now? Are they saving their money or making smart purchases? Are they reading books to educate themselves about financial affairs?

Don't be like these people. Prepare yourself mentally before you get there. Make the commitment to change. It all starts with asking questions.

Lesson 24

"Ask Questions...Lots of Questions."

"One who asks a question is a fool for five minutes; one who does not ask a question remains a fool forever."
– Chinese Proverb

It was my college graduation day. After twelve years of hard work, I was finally walking across the stage to receive my college degree. I wanted to share the moment with the people closest to me, my family.

I was in a theater packed with hundreds of people. Strangely, not seeing my family in the crowd made me feel alone. As I waited for the ceremony to begin, I heard a cheer from the crowd, "hey, Frank!" My brother, sister, and mother were there to support me. My loneliness suddenly left me. The rest of the ceremony was a happy blur. I barely remember getting my diploma. After the ceremony, I was anxious to see my family at the graduate reception. Hugs were exchanged and photos were taken. I noticed my mother had a nervous look on her face after the photos. I asked her if something was wrong. She responded, "there she is!"

I looked over my shoulder to see our commencement speaker, the late Congresswoman Stephanie Tubbs Jones. My mother had seen her deliver a speech at the 2004 Democratic National Convention and was a huge fan. I encouraged my mom to ask her for a photograph. She told me, "I'm too scared to ask. What if she says no?" My mother, the woman I knew as fearless, was lacking the courage to approach someone that she idolized. That's when I told her, "it never hurts to ask... if you don't do it, I will!" "No, I'll do it," she responded.

My pep talk gave her the needed push to introduce herself to the Congresswoman. My mother told her how she admired her and would like a photograph with her. Congresswoman Jones not only obliged, but cheerfully invited all of us over for a group photo.

Soon, everyone noticed the Congresswoman was in the room and approached for their opportunity to take a photo with her. Her assistant informed the gathering crowd that the Congresswoman had another appointment and needed to leave. The last photo she took that day was with my mother. The courage to approach the Congresswoman and ask a simple question created a special moment that we wouldn't forget. Several people approached my mother and made the same comment, "I wish I had the courage to ask for a photograph!" That courage made me proud of my mother.

"Fresh from the Kitchen"

My mother didn't realize it, but she was a leader. She was motivating herself toward living her dream of talking to one of her idols and inspiring her children. Leaders are people of action. Leaders have a drive and passion that unites the people they lead.

Throughout our young lives, my mother taught my brother, sister, and I to work hard towards accomplishing our dreams. It is one thing to speak wisdom, but it is something completely different to *demonstrate wisdom*. Her dream of meeting her idol inspired her children. She showed us that it takes action to accomplish a dream. Her fear did not prevent her from achieving her dream.

My mother's courage was fueled by asking questions. She asked me for my input. Then she asked the congresswoman a question. The ability to gain strength and courage comes from our ability to ask questions. A.S.K. means to Always Seek Knowledge! That's what I preach with my good friend and professional speaker Rodger Campbell. Leaders ask questions. Successful leaders accomplish their dreams faster, smarter, and with less mistakes when they take the time to ask questions.

People make mistakes, but the point is not to repeat mistakes. By asking questions, people can avoid mistakes and pitfalls. People fear asking questions for a variety of reasons. The key to asking questions is working up the courage to ask. It is important to realize that asking questions can only get you closer to your dreams. You never lose ground when asking questions.

You either stay in the same place or advance forward. You can advance forward by asking these three questions.

1. What do I want?
2. What is its value to me?
3. How do I get it?

Dreams are what we want and need. I always suggest that individuals or organizations write down all of their dreams on a piece of paper. Did you write your "Grocery List" earlier in this book? When you were writing or drawing your list, did you dream the big dream? If you didn't, here is your second chance to write down everything you ever dreamed of doing on a piece of paper. Don't limit yourself. Write down needs and wants. After you've completed the list, look at it. Now ask yourself, "what do I really value?" You can also ask, "why is it valuable and important to me?" Finally, you need to ask the final question, "what do I do to make my dreams come true?" The answer is simple. Ask questions. There are no stupid questions. However, it is possible to ask the wrong questions or worse, not asking questions at all.

The most important question you can ask is, "Do I need help?" The courage to admit that you need help is very important. You must recognize that you cannot do everything yourself. Every successful person is surrounded by a team to support them. Surround yourself with good people and listen to their ideas.

"Fresh from the Kitchen"

Successful people surround themselves with people they trust and can turn to for advice; these are people who aren't afraid to tell you that you are heading down the wrong path, or to tell you that there is something that you may have overlooked something that will assist in making the dream become reality. Asking for help is the ability to delegate. It is the ability to value the dream coming true versus thinking you are better than everyone else.

No matter how new or fresh the dream, someone has been there before or had a similar experience. There are people who have been successful at accomplishing dreams similar to yours. These people aren't any better than you. They are just a little further down the trail of success. Research, learn about, and find these people. Use social media and technology to contact and communicate with them.

When you meet these people, take time to ask questions. Be sure to explain your dream. Then, ask questions to discover the obstacles that may deter you from accomplishing your dreams. Ask questions help you achieve your dreams. The courage to ask questions comes from the belief that you have in your dream. Without belief, there is no reality.

Lesson 25

"You are a Super Hero."

"Who has confidence in himself will gain the confidence of others." – Lieb Lazarow

You are a Super Hero! It may be hard to believe, but it's true.

You are a super hero because you possess abilities and talents that people are jealous of. You are unique. You are special. Your abilities and talents can be used for good. You have the ability to help people around the world. The only question is, "do you have a super hero costume?"

Every Super Hero has a costume. They come from different parts of the globe, from different planets, and some even come from different dimensions. Super Heroes have a variety of superpowers that others don't have. They have different beliefs and purposes. Some Super Heroes are simply different. The one thing they do have in common is a costume. They have costumes or uniforms that give them confidence. The costumes give them confidence to display their abilities.

"Fresh from the Kitchen"

Many people lack the confidence to showcase their talents and abilities. Many times, this lack of confidence is based on appearance. Have you ever lacked confidence because you didn't like the way you looked? Has anyone ever told you to be comfortable in your own skin?

A Super Hero's confidence comes from their costume. I am sure that you can think of several Super Heroes that do *super* things once they're in a costume. As their alter ego, they don't showcase their special abilities. They lack confidence. In their costume, anything is possible. That brings me to you.

I'm known for wearing the color green on stage or when I'm working. Green is the color of Life, Growth and Action. 3 powerful subjects I speak on. Every time I wear green I am empowered. It is a visual reminder of my mission in life. Do you have clothing that makes you feel powerful? Do you have a power suit? You know, that suit you wear when you go for that big interview.

I was not a big fan of fashion growing up. A t-shirt and jeans were just fine for me. As I got older, my mom constantly bothered (encouraged) me about the importance of making a great first impression. She told me that I needed to watch how I dress. She was right; I needed to dress more professionally. I would be treated like a child if I dressed like one. I wanted to be a part of the professional world, so I really needed to look the part.

"Fresh from the Kitchen"

I hated getting dressed up. Everything felt uncomfortable. The more uncomfortable I felt, the less confidence I had. I needed help. Franco and Dominic Terriaco were my saviors. The brothers run *Terriaco Suit and Tailoring* in Mentor, Ohio. They treated me like family. They educated me on how to dress. I was taught about quality. I was shown how clothing should properly fit. They showed me what clothes worked best for me. It's amazing how much confidence you gain when you look at yourself in the mirror and feel good about what you are wearing.

In order for you to accomplish your dreams, you need confidence. Call it confidence or superstition, there are endless stories about people wearing a favorite article of clothing to give them confidence. Athletes wear special socks. A woman may wear her favorite shoes. Businessmen wear power ties. Actors wear their favorite color. Bruce Wayne becomes *Batman* by putting on a mask and suit. These are all examples of clothing making the man or woman.

Look in your closet: what clothing makes you feel good about yourself? What gives you confidence? These items are your Super Hero costumes. They give you confidence, strength, and the ability to take on the world. You must have the proper mindset to pursue your dreams. My fashion education made me feel like I could take on the world. Anytime I went into a meeting or an interview my attire gave me confidence. To this day, Franco and Dominic are still advising me on what I should and shouldn't wear when I stop by to visit their store in Ohio.

"Fresh from the Kitchen"

When you need assistance putting together the perfect wardrobe, contact the brothers. They will show you how to dress with confidence for any occasion or event. They teach you how to create a style that matches your personality with your body type. Tell them that Frankie sent you.

Lesson 26

"Take care of Yourself...Physically and Mentally."

"Busy means something else is more important."
– Frank Kitchen

Are you looking out for number one? It is an important, thought- provoking question. The question popped into my head one night when I finally did something to take care of myself. I was getting a massage through the massage therapy program at Lakeland Community College. The program looks for volunteers their students can work on. The massages were relaxing. They work out the kinks in muscles that I didn't know existed.

While I was lying face down on the table, I started thinking about how an hour of *me time* would help out in several areas of my life. The thoughts came from a handout one of my good friends had shared with me. It listed things people should do to live productive and healthy lives. There were comments about healthy eating, finances, and natural living. I was drawn to two bullet points.

- Dedicate at least one hour to yourself daily.
- Stress is linked to the six leading causes of death: heart disease, cancer, lung ailments, accidents, liver cirrhosis, and suicide.

"Fresh from the Kitchen"

My friend told me that he rarely does anything to take care of himself. He put a lot of his time and energy into work and other

endeavors. He was stressed, run down, and unmotivated. He said: "I really need to take care of myself, I don't have the energy to spend time with my wife and kids." His family was his number one priority, but he wasn't living that way. We started to talk, and I asked him what he did for himself. This is a question that I've asked a lot of people I work with.

While speaking at a conference, I listened to health expert Deanna Latson make a great comment: "People spend more time taking care of their homes, cars, material items, and work than themselves. You can get a new job and new possessions, but you only get one body!"

That really made me think. You can't have healthy relationships, possessions, or live your dreams, if you don't take care of yourself. If you're not healthy mentally or physically you won't be able to take care of yourself or the people you care about.

Your life is the most important thing that you possess. Many fail to think this way. People put more time and effort into work than themselves. They hoard vacation time while making comments like, "I can't take a vacation because I'll have a ton of work to do when I get back." You must remove stress and negatives from your life. De-stress before your unpleasant mood and actions poorly affect the relationships you have with the people closest to you. When you don't rest, you perform poorly at work and other activities that are important to you.

When you don't maintain your health, you can't be there for your spouse, significant other, family, or friends. It all comes back to taking proper care of your body and yourself.

Isn't it amazing how people will treat cars better than themselves? People service their car regularly, but won't take time to go in for a check-up at the doctor. They'll get their car washed and detailed, but won't take care of their body.

I hope that reading this will encourage you to take time to figure out what you can do for yourself to make yourself happier, stress-free, healthier, motivated, and positive. You can't do anything for others if you're not around. Once you take care of yourself, you'll have a better chance of achieving all of your hopes and dreams. For people who say they are too busy or don't have time, think about the following:

People make time to watch their favorite television shows, but can't make time to exercise.

People get premium gasoline for their cars, but buy second-rate food to put in their stomachs.

People constantly say that they are too busy, then complain that they can't do the things that are important to them.

"Fresh from the Kitchen"

Busy means something else is more important at the time. When something is truly important, you will make time for it. Life is short, do what you can to enjoy it, and live it to the best of your abilities. Take care of yourself and take care of the one thing you'll only get one of... you!

What do you need to do to properly maintain your mental and physical health?

Lesson 27

"Practice What You Preach!"

"It's not fair to ask of others what you are not willing to do yourself." – *Elenor Roosevelt*

I'm a huge believer that God tests us to see if we will practice what we preach. My wife calls this karma. People listen to our actions more than our words. I was challenged to live what I wrote in the previous chapter in 2019. I discovered I wasn't taking care of my health as well as I thought I was. This is a post I shared with my social media followers to encourage people to take care of their health.

June 22, 2019 - Facebook

There are times when many of us share only "part of the truth" on Facebook or social media. We share the fun stuff but not the real stuff. You don't have to tell all of your business, but there are other times when sharing a truthful transparent nugget can motivate you and others.

In March of 2019, my wife and I visited Back to Health of Anthem to do a health screening with Dr. Brian Hester. I assumed my health was really good other than needing to gain weight.

"Fresh from the Kitchen"

When the results came back, I discovered that my health wasn't terrible but it was really good either. I was underweight (no surprise), had issues with my cholesterol (surprise) and on the verge of being pre diabetic (huge surprise).

Kelly and I enrolled in the 8 weeks to Wellness program to improve our overall health. It wasn't an 8 week program, it was eight weeks to learn how to develop habits, thoughts, behaviors and actions to improve our health for the rest of our lives.

I don't like talking about my weight because I've always been embarrassed about it and I was picked on for being "skinny" when I was growing up. If I shared my issues with gaining healthy weight or keeping weight on, comments of "must be nice" or making others feel insecure about their weight/weight issues kept me quiet. People worry about being overweight, but did you know being underweight can cause health issues too?

When I speak, I often ask my audiences to write this down, "If you're afraid to share your dream, then you're afraid to live your dream!" I shared my dream with Brian's team. In a little over 8 weeks, almost all of my major health concerns improved. I was told I was the first person at their office to score an A on my follow up Wellness score? Why did this happen? I changed my thoughts, habits, behaviors and actions. I made my health dream important. It's one thing to say something is important to you. It's another to show how important something is to you.

"Fresh from the Kitchen"

I committed to changing my diet and working out, including doing leg workouts! I knew I had to change. I want to be around for my wife and kids as long and healthy as possible. Success is about living your dream, your passion, or your purpose. You can't live it, if you don't make it important. Success isn't about what you know, it's about what you do...it's about the actions you take and choices you make.

For years, I've struggled with my weight and health differently than most. I've wanted to change, but I kept a lot to myself because I worried about what others would think. I was creating mental barriers and excuses that became physical roadblocks.

If you look at the top of the posted photo, you'll see it says my weight started at 157lbs. To be honest, I got the flu right after my weigh in and dropped to 150lbs! Not good when you're 6'2. The first couple of weeks, I struggled to gain weight then lost what I gained. Then I fully committed to what I was being taught. I finished the program just under 161lbs. I gained over 10lbs of muscle while dropping my body fat %. All of my blood sugar and cholesterol issues are gone. But that's not my long term dream. My ideal weight is between 170-175 healthy lbs. I'm not there yet. That wasn't possible in 8 weeks. A lifetime of choices can't be corrected that fast.

This is my dream, something I feel I can do before my birthday in September. 175lbs by 9/4/19 to celebrate my 46th birthday... and to keep everything in the green the rest of my life.

"Fresh from the Kitchen"

I'm sharing this dream, because I've been afraid to live it for over 45 years! I'm sharing, so everyone reading this can be my accountability partner.

I can do the same for you too. What is the big dream you're looking to live? Don't be ashamed of it. Share it with someone (including me) who is willing to support you and push you to live it.

I want to thank the Back to Health Team. I still have a lot of work to do, especially on the flexibility part of my health. I'll keep posting updates on FB and Instagram to let people know my progress. Thank you for reading and please remember this, your thoughts, habits, behaviors and actions (choices) can create or prevent your success (living your dream). If you're unwilling to change any of the four then don't expect to see the results your hoping, wishing or dreaming of. You can do it! Good Luck with whatever your big dream is! I'm off to work out....

Lesson 28

"Take a Vacation!"

"I need a vacation" – countless people worldwide

Have you caught yourself saying the line above over and over again? I have. Anytime I catch myself saying those words, I go on a vacation. You can too. You're probably saying, "I can't afford to go on a vacation." Or, you might be saying, "I don't have the time to take a vacation." You're also thinking, "Frank must have a lot of money." The answers are simple. Yes, you can afford a vacation. Yes, you have the time to take a vacation. No, I don't have a lot of money...yet. You don't need a lot of money, but you need to know the meaning of the word vacation.

Vacation is defined as a period of recreation. Recreation is defined as an activity done for enjoyment when one is not working. Simply put, a vacation is a time for you to enjoy yourself by not working. What are some of the things you can do to enjoy life?

Life is a wonderful thing. It is something to enjoy. You can't spend it all working. You need time to recharge your battery. You need time to turn your brain off and enjoy yourself. This is why people flock to comedy films at the movie theater. Critics will give poor reviews to *silly* and *childish* movies that become the most popular and profitable movies of the year.

Why does this occur? People need recreation. People need time to de-stress their bodies and minds. The human body is an amazing machine. As with any machine, it can be overworked, overused and over stressed. You can give it brief or extended periods of time off. Some people think extended time off is the only way – this is not true. A brief break can do wonders for your body.

Earlier in this book, I asked you to write a list of your wants and needs on a lifetime grocery list. Did you write them down? I am sure that there were activities on your list that cost money. I am betting that there are a few activities that don't cost money. This means that you can afford to take a vacation. Any period of time can be a vacation. People have just been programmed to think a vacation has to last several days. People believe you can only call it a vacation when you leave town. Time in the park reading a book can be classified as a vacation. It's recreation. It's time away from work. It's something you can do to enjoy life.

This is where you say, "I don't have time to read a book." You also say, "I don't have time to take a vacation." Wrong and wrong! First, you're reading this book. Thank you! Second, you make time for what you want. Stop using the excuse, "I'm too busy." Busy means something else is more important. Anything you find important you have to make time for. Just like a long vacation, you need to write *short vacation* times on your calendar.

"Fresh from the Kitchen"

When you write vacation on your calendar, everything gets put on hold. Your vacation is important and you have made time for it. Give yourself a daily vacation. Set a reminder on your phone. Even if it's only for a few minutes, it will be good for you and your health.

Going on a vacation puts you in a positive mental state. The moment you begin your vacation, everything about you is positive. You smile more. Your body language is out of this world. Your confidence is sky high. You are relaxed and ready to enjoy yourself. Wouldn't that mindset and feeling be great to have all the time? You can have it – just by changing your mindset.

You have to recognize that you need to take time to enjoy yourself, no matter how short or long the period of time. You must realize that this is the true definition of a vacation. You need to acknowledge that you don't need a lot of money to take a vacation. There are countless forms of recreational activities you can do that cost little or no money. Finally, you have to establish set times for you to vacation. Once you put something on your calendar, your mindset changes. Vacations are important to you. Once you're on vacation, it's the only thing you are thinking about. You're not thinking about work. You're not thinking about the stresses of your life. You're just enjoying yourself.

Happy vacationing. Feel free to send me pictures of you on your vacation. It will make your vacation feel more real and I'll be excited to see you enjoying yourself. You can email me at FRESH@FRANKKITCHEN.COM

Lesson 29

"Maintain your Excellence."

"To achieve the results you are proud of, you must practice Excellence." - Frank Kitchen

Excellence is the ability to be extremely good and outstanding. Showcasing your excellence is something to be proud of. The world tells us to be perfect. Perfection is something that can never be achieved. There has never been a perfect human being. There have been humans who have been remembered for their excellence at a particular activity or endeavour.

It's difficult to be excellent when you fail to practice excellence in the way you take care of yourself. Here are 7 self-care excellence techniques I share with the leaders I'm invited to work with.

Physical Excellence - Take care of your Body! Health, Nutrition, and Rest

- Take walks and exercise regularly.
- Learning new physical activities... Dancing, Rock Climbing, Yoga
- Get the proper amount of sleep daily… 6-8 hours
- Eat nourishing foods… At home and at work
- Drink water and stay hydrated

Mental Excellence - Learn New Things and apply what you have learned to your daily life including; Self-motivation Activities, Being creative, and Stepping out of your Comfort Zone.

- Being respectful and mindful of yourself and others
- Avoid being judgmental
- Journal and read often (Audio books and Podcasts Count)
- Avoid perfectionism
- Make time for yourself on your calendar...vacation & personal time.
- Schedule regular technology detox periods
- Reward yourself for your achievements

Emotional Excellence - Understand how your emotions, behaviors, habits and actions impact your personal and professional success.

- Learn to say, "No"
- Practice Emotional Intelligence and Empathy
- Practice Gratitude
- Make time to self reflect on how your emotions impact your actions

Social Excellence - Have a supportive community of people you trust. Family, friends & mentors who support, challenge, and empower you.

- Participate in social & professional communities outside of work
- Show up for the commitments you make
- Ask for help or advice
- Grow your community by meeting new people.
- Meet up for walks, hikes or physical activities with your community

Professional Excellence - Share and receive gifts (time, talents, and treasures) with your co-workers and community.

- Express your wants and needs via positive communication
- Have clear and defined boundaries
- Know your limits, role and responsibilities
- Seek out Professional Development & Coaching Opportunities

Environmental Excellence - Create and environment that promotes comfort, confidence and productivity.

- Monitor and limit distractions (technology, people and shiny objects)
- Keep work space and schedule decluttered and well organized. Clean up after yourself.

Environmental Excellence (Continued)

- Maintain excellent grooming standards (Clean clothes and personal hygiene)
- Keep your environment safe. Regular maintenance on transportation, living space and workspaces.

Spiritual Excellence - Have beliefs and values that are important to you and guide you to be your best.

- Practice Prayer, Meditation or Reflection Time
- Volunteer and offer help to those in need
- Journal and read often
- Set goals and share them with people you trust
- Plan/Attend Retreats or Spiritual Getaways

Lesson 30

"Every Experience in Life is Learning Opportunity."

"Nothing is a waste of time if you use the experience wisely."
– Auguste Rodin

I was an "accidental model." I was *discovered* while spending a night out on the town with my friends. We were at a nightclub having a good time when several very tall and attractive women approached us.

My friends magically disappeared. I felt as if I were being sacrificed. I discovered that the women were model scouts. They told me that I had a *good look* and should consider being a model. I immediately began looking for video cameras, because I knew a practical joke was being played on me. Fortunately for me, it was not a joke. I was given an invitation for an audition and the women left. As if by magic, my friends re-appeared to interrogate me. They had a hard time believing the offer, too. I put the invitation in my back pocket and I continued to enjoy the night with my friends.

The full story of how I got into the world of professional modeling will have to be written in another book. The stories are funny, but the lessons I learned have been very important.

"Fresh from the Kitchen"

Working as a Model taught me a lot about life and myself. One day, I'll be able to show my kids how Dad used to be cool. They will probably laugh and say "yeah, right!" That's when I will share the story of how I was an underwear model. On second thought, I will wait to tell them this story when they're in their thirties.

My adventure as an underwear model began when I was invited to model for a runway show. I was scheduled to model several outfits. Most were cool, and I wanted to keep some of the clothes that I was scheduled to wear. The charity event was being held to raise money for *Rainbow Babies and Children's Hospital*.

Every runway show required that the models attend a dress rehearsal. The rehearsals were held to practice routines and guarantee clothes fit properly. During the practice, one of my fellow models re-aggravated a back injury. Feel free to insert a joke here. The model was my friend Ryan. He was scheduled to participate in a routine where he would carry a female model. She would be in lingerie and he would be shirtless while wearing pants. After he was injured, I was told that I would be filling in for him.

I am not the biggest guy in the world, and being shirtless in front of a crowd made me very nervous and self-conscious. There were only so many push-ups that I could do at the last second to look bigger. Things got worse when I was told the routine was being changed. They decided to change the wardrobe. Part of me thought "yes!" Then, terror struck when I found out that I would be wearing only very small boxer briefs in public!

"Yes!" I would be showing off my push-ups enhanced chest and my chicken legs. Did I mention the briefs had a lion on the front? The words *Roar* were written just above the lion. Very classy!

The show was going great when my number was called. The events were a blur. I remember hearing applause. I remember not dropping the half dressed model that sat on my shoulder. At the after party, several members of the audience came up to me. They made comments about me being the *underwear guy.* I thought the worst until I heard a sincere "you looked good!"

The experience was funny. It was also very educational. There will be moments in our lives when we will look back at an embarrassing moment and reflect. We will recognize how much we learned from that experience. Do you have any embarrassing life experiences you have learned from?

Here are a few things I learned from my experience

"Practice, Practice, Practice."

There is a science to walking the runway. It's not as easy as it looks. Every runway show that I have ever participated in had a rehearsal. It was an opportunity to practice. The more you practice, the better you get. I had to walk through my routines multiple times. I didn't want to fall off the catwalk. I needed to practice good habits. The walk-through gave me the opportunity to learn and improve.

"Embarrassing moments will happen."

You may not be caught in your underwear, but life is full of experiences you and others will find embarrassing. Take ownership of that experience. Live in the moment and use that moment to gain confidence.

"Everything in life is a growth opportunity."

Even embarrassing moments can be used to gain strength and confidence. I can do almost anything in life now because hundreds of people saw me in my underwear. Nothing else in my life will be more embarrassing than that. Each time I fear something, I reflect back on that moment and the fear goes away and the laughter begins.

"Don't run away from challenges."

I had the opportunity to turn down my "underwear moment." My dream was to be a successful model. Runway shoes and stepping out of my comfort zone are part of the job description. After the show, several opportunities opened up for me. I was invited to be in more shows. I made great contacts that led to more work. None of that would have happened if I ran away from the challenge. When we run away from our fears, we are really running away from our dreams. Challenges are put into our life to prove how badly we want something.

"Always start on the right foot."

When walking on the runway, models are always taught to start with their right foot. You always want to take the right steps. Life is the same way: be sure to start the right way. People rarely get second chances or opportunities to do something. Make every moment count. Have confidence and look confident. Make a great first impression. Enjoy the moment and don't rush it. Take your time. I wanted to run down that runway as quickly as possible. Had I done that, I would have dropped the "lingerie angel" sitting on my shoulders. I had to stand up straight, be confident, walk slowly, and start with the right foot. I was nervous, but I didn't give that impression to the crowd. It showed, because several of the models said: "I couldn't have done that, you looked so confident."

"Celebrate."

After every show, there is a party. Parties are held to celebrate the night's accomplishments. Participants talk about what went right, share memorable moments, build relationships, talk about the future, and enjoy turning a vision into reality. My celebration was displayed by the smile on my face. I celebrated my personal growth. The shy kid from high school just walked a runway in his underwear and lived to tell the story.

Lesson 31

"Plan for Emergencies."

"Dream as if you'll live forever, live as if you'll die today."
- James Dean

The death of a loved one is never easy. I've had several people close to me loose a loved one. Some were expected and others were unexpected. When a death happens, what do you say to put one's mind at ease? If I were in their shoes, would I want my loved one to pass away unexpectedly, or would I want to know exactly when things would end?

I started thinking about death when I had to have my living will and durable power of attorney notarized for my Rotary Trip to Australia. It's scary to think that I was preparing for my eventual death, but I also felt good that the people closest to me would know what to do when that day happens. They would know what my wishes were. We hear so many stories of people suddenly dying and no one knowing what to do; hearing these stories really got me thinking about my will.

While I was preparing my will, I heard a story of a U.S. serviceman who passed away in Iraq. He had been writing his family constantly via email. Due to privacy laws, the family was unable to get into his email account to collect the emails that they had exchanged. After six months of non- usage, the e-mail account was deleted.

It made me think, "do the people closest to me know where I keep my important information?" and "do they know what my wishes are if I were to pass away unexpectedly?"

I began to put together an emergency file on my computer. I started collecting all my passwords for everything, all of my account information, phone numbers, and contact information of my friends and family. I put together lists of where to find things in my apartment. All of my planning helped me realize how much the people closest to me didn't know about me. It was scary. I thought about how tough things would really be if I had passed away. Death isn't an easy thing, but I'd like it to be somewhat easier for the people closest to me. After I completed my list, I made copies. I gave them to the people that I trusted.
The copies were put into envelopes that said "open in case of an emergency." My mind was at ease because I knew my family and friends wouldn't be on the news fighting with the government or a hospital because no one knew what to do.

I hope that I didn't scare you. I wrote this as a reflection piece. Do the people closest to you really know you? How well do you really know the people closest to you? What are your wishes in case there is an unexpected emergency? There are a lot of businesses that have an emergency plan. Do you and your loved ones have one?

In loving memory of

Richard A. Cummings June 9, 1938 – October 12, 2009
Cornelius Mack - July 23,1925 - January 6, 2016

Lesson 32

"Share your Wisdom and Talents with the World."

"Why be the King or Queen of the Mountain if you have no one to share the view with?" - Kelly Duran

When I worked at Lakeland Community College, I had the opportunity to work with some phenomenal students. They truly impacted my life in positive ways. This chapter is about one of those phenomenal students.

One Spring day, I walked into my office and found a nice surprise waiting for me. There was a handmade Yoda statue on my desk. It had the following inscription on the bottom:

To Frank:
Thanks for all you do. Great Friend, you are. May the Force be with you! Amelia

It was made by one of the students who worked for me. She is a huge Star Wars fan. She gave me the Yoda for assisting her transfer to another school. My students and co-workers knew that I was a *Star Wars* fan too. A few called me Yoda. They often teased me by saying, "You share your wisdom, but you can be hard to understand!"

"Fresh from the Kitchen"

Amelia was off to film school, but found the time to make a gift and bring it to my office. She told me that my "Yoda Award" was a sign of appreciation for all the help I gave. I told Amelia that I expected to see her name on the big screen someday. Truth be told, I am confident that she will win an Oscar some day. When I see her win her award, I'll be sure to look at my "Yoda Award" and smile.

There were days that I wondered why I did my job at the college. Then, special days like that one occurred. Never forget to share your wisdom, knowledge, talents and experiences with the people around you. You may not receive a physical award, but you will be rewarded. I love volunteering, because everyone involved grows. You have the ability to make the world a better place. By sharing, you positively impact your life and the lives of others.

I recently re-connected with Amelia via Facebook. She is living near Hollywood and working in the film industry. I let her know that I still have my award and how special it is to me. Here's what she wrote me:

"Fresh from the Kitchen"

Thank you for embracing Yoda all these years. That really meant a lot to me to know that he is traveling the country with you.

Please let me know when you will be in town. And also, let me know how that book is coming along. You inspired many of us back in Ohio.

Amelia

In 2019, I reconnected with Amelia and her Husband over lunch. A few months later we worked together at a Fundraising Event to positively impact the lives of Families being assisted by the March of Dimes.

What knowledge or talent can you share with the world?

Who can you share your knowledge with?

What groups would you like to volunteer with?

Lesson 33

"Communication is the Key to Everything."

"Communication works for those who work at it."
– John Powell

My visit to Australia in 2006 was a life changing adventure.

The memories are still burned into my thoughts. I talk about my adventures whenever the opportunity arises. One of my favorite experiences was my scuba diving adventure at the Great Barrier Reef.

Our ability to communicate in an understandable way is the determining factor to positive or negative experiences. Poor communication can lead to misunderstandings. Misunderstandings lead to communication breakdowns. Lack of communication limits growth.

I was in the resort town of Cairns, Australia. I had just completed my Rotary Group Study Exchange. I wanted to experience more of Australia, so I arranged to stay in the country for an extra week. Cairns is located near the Great Barrier Reef. It was something that I needed to see. My plan was to find a local charter boat to take me to the reef. I wanted to snorkel and take pictures.

"Fresh from the Kitchen"

I spoke with the locals. They told me to go to the marina to investigate which charter company I should use. The tourist books all recommended the same charters. I went against their recommendations and selected a smaller charter company. When I approached their desk, the employees greeted me with huge smiles on their faces. I was treated as someone special from the first moment. They clearly explained to me how the tours worked. I was told to show up to the marina the next morning and be prepared to have a fun day

When I arrived at the marina the next morning, I was ready to go. A fleet of charter boats filled up with hundreds of tourists. Many of the boats were overflowing. My boat had only twenty tourists. The boat was designed to hold one hundred people. The crew greeted us as we boarded. After a safety meeting, we were on our way.

It took two hours to get to the reef. The weather was perfect and the views of the ocean and mainland were spectacular. When we arrived, the crew asked who wanted to snorkel and who wanted to scuba dive. I planned to snorkel until one of the crew asked me, "Don't you want to scuba?" I responded, "I'm not certified." They told me that they could train me. This is when I remembered my grocery list. Three particular items jumped out:

- ❑ I will visit Australia
- ❑ I will visit the Great Barrier Reef
- ❑ I will go scuba diving

"Fresh from the Kitchen"

It was time for me to cross several items off of my grocery list. I was fitted for a wetsuit. I was fitted for all of my scuba gear. I went through a brief class on how to scuba dive, how to use my equipment, dangers to avoid, and how to communicate underwater.

Yes, communicate. We wouldn't be able to talk with our instructor underwater, so we were taught a series of hand gestures.

Some of the gestures were as follows:

Thumbs up meant that I wanted to return to the surface.

Thumbs down meant that I was ok to go deeper.

Putting my thumb and index finger together to make a circle and holding my other three fingers straight up meant that everything was ok.

If I wanted to go in a certain direction, I was supposed to point to my eyes first. Then I was supposed to point in the direction that I wanted to go. Next, I would wait for the ok sign from my instructor.

Putting my hands on top of each other and clasping my fingers together with my thumbs out wiggling meant that I saw a sea turtle.
Holding my hand in front of my face with my thumb touching my nose meant that I saw a clown fish.

"Fresh from the Kitchen"

Holding my hand against my forehead with my fingers sticking up like a fin meant that I saw a shark.

My first dive went well. I was underwater for over thirty minutes. I was diving with an underwater camera that I purchased for my adventure. I took pictures of everything, including myself. When I was directed to return to the surface, I was a little sad. I wished that I had had more time.

As I got back on the boat, my guides asked about my adventure. I told them it was great. Then they asked me another question, "Do you want to do it again?" It took me half a second to say yes. The boat went to a new location on the reef and I was back in the water again.

During the dive, I saw a giant sea turtle. I notified my instructor. I was given approval to swim near it and take a picture. I saw a giant clam and followed the same procedure. Then, I saw a clown fish. I alerted my instructor and I got a reaction that I didn't expect. Her eyes got large and huge amounts of bubbles came from her respirator. She shook her head no. I asked again and my instructor began looking around frantically. This is when I realized that I was giving the gesture for shark. We were in an area where sharks lived and the instructor's job was to keep us safe.

After recognizing my mistakes, I waved my hands and made the proper gesture for clown fish. I pointed in the direction of the clownfish. My instructors' faces communicated relief. I took my picture and finished my dive.

When we returned to the boat, we laughed about my miscommunication. My instructor said that it was easy to confuse the gestures when you get excited. She then gave me a great piece of advice, "think before you say something."

Communication isn't just verbal. People communicate verbally and non-verbally. People can write to communicate. Ideas and emotions can be communicated via voice tone and body language. Eye contact can display a variety of feelings. Communication is a skill people possess and use every day. Sadly, it is not something we work on everyday.

There are countless studies that say that *80% of all communication is non-verbal.* You will spend your entire life communicating with other people. This can be done face to face, via email, by text message, video chats, over the telephone, or through hand gestures. Being an effective communicator greatly affects your ability to accomplish your dreams.

Communication is the process of successfully exchanging information, feelings, or ideas from a sender to a receiver. If one or both of the parties performs poorly during the process, misunderstandings will occur.

In this time of emails, smart telephones, text messages, and social media, communication isn't getting better. In fact, it is getting more difficult to understand.

To improve your communication skills, I recommend the three tactics on the next two pages.

1. Don't let technology be a crutch.

Humans are social creatures. Technology has facilitated and impeded our social abilities. It's easy to use technology, but technology doesn't allow a person to display emotion or other non-verbal forms of communication. At some point, you have to meet other people face-to-face. There will be no keyboard or keypad to assist you. Make the time to talk to friends and family in person. Create opportunities to be in the presence of other humans. The more you practice, the better you will become.

2. Take an Interpersonal Communication class.

When I was in college, *Public Speaking 101* was a requirement to graduate. Supposedly, I would learn to be a more effective communicator. That was false. The class teaches you how to speak in public. Speaking in public is the number one fear of people. Most people will never speak in front of a large group in their life.

When I started working at Lakeland Community College, I told all of the students to take *Interpersonal Communication 101.*

I took the same class when I was a student. The class truly taught me how to communicate. My instructor, Barbra McEachern, was amazing. She told her students that we would communicate with others the rest of our life. She taught her students verbal and non-verbal communication.

The students were taught how to communicate one-on-one, in small groups, and in large groups. These are the activities that you'll be participating in your entire life.

3. Take an acting class.

I'm not recommending that you become an actor, but you can learn so much about communication by taking a class or two. In acting, you learn how to display and read emotions. You become competent in the art of communication. You interact with other people. You learn how to display thoughts and emotions verbally and non-verbally. Your practices can be recorded. It is amazing how you may believe you are displaying a certain emotion and your audience reads it differently. Acting is an art and skill, just like communication. The people who are effective are often rewarded.

To learn more about my trip to Australia and see some amazing pictures go to:

http://group6630.blogspot.com, or
www.kitchenfrank.blogspot.com. Click on **April 2006.**

Lesson 34

"Be Prepared to Speak in Public."

"You can write the greatest speech in the world, but it doesn't matter how good it is if you can't deliver it!" - Frank Kitchen

Glossophobia is the fear of public speaking. Many people fear speaking in public more than spiders, snakes, falling out of a plane, clowns and dying! Pretty amazing. Speaking in public can be an amazing experience when you overcome your fear.

You have probably heard that fear is...FALSE EVIDENCE APPEARING REAL. Let me tell you right now, I have never been bitten by a spider or snake while speaking, fallen out of a plane, or had a plane fall on me while speaking. As of writing this book, I haven't died while giving a speech either.

I believe giving a great speech, presentation or communicating in public is all about creating your ideal environment. An environment where you and your audience feel comfortable. I have the honor of volunteering with Hustle PHX in Phoenix, Arizona. **(www.HustlePHX.com)**

The non-profit provides the social, economic and educational resources needed by aspiring entrepreneurs working to live their business dreams. Several times a year, I work with the "Hustlers" to prepare for "Pitch Night." The event is an opportunity for business owners in the program to share the story of their business and their dream with the public. Here are a few of the strategies I share to make your next speech a positive experience.

Take a Field Trip

Learn as much as you can about the location of the speech. Try to visit ahead of time to see how things will be set-up. Ask for details of the location including attendance, type of sound system, and seating arrangements. Ask for practice time. You gain confidence by being comfortable. When you're not comfortable or familiar with the environment, you'll lose your confidence.

Create Your Environment

Show up to your speaking location ahead of time to get comfortable with the space. Set up the location to make you feel comfortable. I recommend you arrive 1 hour before you speak.

Follow Your Routine

Create a pre speech routine. Meditate, pray, listen to music, use the bathroom, etc. You want to create a comfort zone for yourself to be the best you can possibly be on stage.

Eat Smart and Drink Smart

Make smart decisions on what you eat and drink before you speak. I recommend eating nothing heavy 1 hour before you speak. A full stomach makes it difficult to breathe. Your voice is your tool. Drink room temperature water or something warm before you speak. Cold drinks or carbonated beverages have negative effects on your ability to speak. Hard candy or throat lozenges are your friends.

You are a Super Hero

Every Super Hero has their special uniform. Wear what makes you feel great about yourself. Look good feel good. Be confident and own the room.

Smile

Smiling will put you and your audience at ease. Before you speak, think of something enjoyable...your friends, your family, your pet, or something that puts a smile on your face.

Chin Up and Mouth Open

You are difficult to hear when you don't open your mouth and you project your voice towards the floor. When using a microphone, learn how to use it properly.

Share Your Passion

Only speak about subjects or themes you are passionate about. People get nervous when they have to speak about something they don't know about or aren't comfortable with. When you know the subject or the story, all will be good.

Share Your Story

Don't overthink things. People psych themselves out. You're telling a story and sharing information with people. You are having a conversation with the audience. Talk with them, not at them. Don't make it a lecture.

Use Your Words - Only use words that you are comfortable with. Don't **TRY** to sound intelligent by using words that aren't in your normal vocabulary. You'll only stumble over them and get nervous.

Be Yourself – Audiences connect with people who are genuine. If you like to walk around, use slides, and interact with people...do it. Do what makes you feel comfortable. When you are comfortable the audience is comfortable.

Be a Speaker not a Reader - If you have to read your speech, type everything in a large font so you can read the words. I like to color code the lines so I can find my spot when I look up at the audience. Remember the only person who will see your speech is you.

Have Fun! - When you're not enjoying your time on stage then your audience won't enjoy themselves either. Embrace the moment, have a good time and share your story. Share your knowledge. Share your dream.

Looking to improve your public speaking skills? Are you an aspiring professional speaker? Please join my Facebook Group "Spice Up your Speaking" as I share strategies and techniques that took my from shy and nervous to comfortable, confident and highly requested.

Facebook.com/SpiceUpYourSpeaking

Lesson 35

"There will Always be People trying to Kill Your Dreams."

"You are the combined average of the people you hang out with the most." – Jim Rohn

My mother always shared with me the value of hanging out with the right people. It's some of the best advice that a parent can give. We are a reflection of the people we spend the most time with. When you are around people who are chasing after and accomplishing their dreams, then you will achieve your dreams too. When you spend time around positive and productive people, they help insulate you from the negativity and dream crushing possibilities the world can throw at you.

Over the years, I have learned that there will always be haters, people who will try their best to kill your dreams. Owning a business is like riding a rollercoaster. There are lots of ups and downs. Operating your own business requires a lot of dedication, focus, motivation and perseverance.

Many people get to see the fun side of my business on social media and in person. Only a select few get to see the not so fun stuff needed to run my business...contract negotiations, financial paperwork, legalese, phone calls, travel delays and staying in a cornucopia of hotels.

"Fresh from the Kitchen"

I do what I do because I want to take care of my family and help people and organizations around the world become positive difference makers and life changers. I work hard to keep myself around positive people and positive environments.

These actions help insulate me from the negativity society bombards us with daily. It's my negativity force field. What do you do to protect yourself from negativity?

When Frank Kitchen Enterprises celebrated its first anniversary as a full-time business, I experienced a moment of negativity. You know what I'm talking about, a moment that can ruin your day. I was contacting potential clients about speaking opportunities. I was lucky enough to get in contact with someone who really "loved" their job. The gentlemen took it upon himself to share his "love" of his job with me. He let me know that I needed to get a real job and give up professional speaking as a career. He let me know that youth don't like speakers and they forget the message of the speaker before they get off the stage.

I attempted several times to get off the phone by thanking him for his advice, but he just kept "sharing" his advice and honesty with me. The comment I loved the most was when he asked, "Am I making you cry?" several times. I think I upset him when I replied, "no I'm not crying." I finally managed to end the call.

I could have let my phone experience ruin my day or rethink my choice to be a business owner, but I didn't. Why? Negative experiences are going to happen. How we deal with these experiences determines how successful we can be.

"Fresh from the Kitchen"

Success is the ability to live a dream, your dream. The ability to live your passion or purpose. The people I surround myself with and the environments I choose to be in greatly affect my ability to deal with negative experiences.

After ending the call, I spoke with several of my brothers and sisters in the professional speaking world. They all gave me the same pep talk, "Don't allow him to pass his negativity onto you. There are people in the world who only feel better by making someone else feel worse than them." I got back to work making more phone calls and replying to emails. I smiled when I received several positive messages from students and professionals who attended my events that year and remembered my message. I smiled even bigger when I received two emails from organizations requesting information on how to book me for their upcoming events.

When you have a dream you want to live, don't allow someone who doesn't know you, care about you, or possess a negative attitude to determine how you feel about yourself and your pursuits. When you place yourself in an environment with a positive culture with productive people, you'll be able to deal with negativity in a positive and productive way.

Lesson 36

"Life is a Jigsaw Puzzle."

"You are a part of someone's life. You may never know where you fit, but someone's life may never be complete without you in it." - Unknown

Have you ever had the pleasure or aggravation of putting together a jigsaw puzzle? They come in different sizes and forms. Some can be put together really fast and others take longer. Work and focus are required to put the pieces together. On the front of every puzzle box is a picture. It's the completed vision shared with you by the manufacturer. The box contains all the pieces to complete the puzzle. It's up to you to recognize how all of the pieces fit together to make the vision a reality.

Life is one complicated jigsaw puzzle. When you shop for a puzzle at a store, you search for a picture that appeals to you. You pick the vision that you would like to put together. Life is the same way. It will take time, but eventually you discover a vision you would like to see become reality.

The best way to assemble a puzzle is to work backwards. First, we need a vision or mission. Have you ever tried to assemble a puzzle when you didn't have the box? Just thinking about this makes me want to scream, but that's life.

"Fresh from the Kitchen"

Remember the chapter on Mission Statements? When you don't have a vision of a completed puzzle, it becomes difficult to assemble the puzzle. Once you have a vision, you open the box, spread out all of the pieces and find a place to start working. Look at all the pieces to see what you have. At first glance, the puzzle pieces can be confusing. The activity appears to be overwhelming, but as you're sorting through them, you start to notice how pieces fit together. Eventually, you start to piece together the vision.

Life is the sorting period for our vision. You have many pieces to sort through. This can be very frustrating. As you attempt to put the pieces together, you experience successes and failures. You don't give up because you want to see the completed vision. You want your vision to become reality. Eventually, you have that "light bulb moment" where you *see* everything differently. The pieces start to go together easier. You recognize how they are supposed to fit together. Before you know it, the puzzle is complete.

To complete the puzzle of life, you have to focus on all of the relationships and experiences in your life. Take the time to notice how they fit together. Everything that happens to you in life can be used to learn and grow. This process can be frustrating, but life is a jigsaw puzzle. Once you recognize that everything that happens in your life is a piece of the puzzle, you must create a plan to sort the pieces and assemble them. There will be successes and failures, but like assembling a puzzle, some pieces fit while others don't.

You must learn from your mistakes in order to avoid repeating them. You have to adjust and try again. Eventually, you will have that "light bulb moment." You will know what pieces you need to find. You will know how they fit together. You will start to assemble them and you will complete your puzzle. It will take time, perhaps a lifetime.

There will be times when you may focus only on specific areas of the puzzle. But, in your mind, you will know that you're working to complete your grand vision.

Lesson 37

"Find Something or Someone to Fall in Love With."

"Life is like a puzzle, when you find the heart of the puzzle, the rest will complete itself" - Joshua Vander Linden

As a child, I constantly dreamed about everything. I wanted to be an astronaut, a professional football player, a city planner, a businessman, an Olympian, a movie star, and someone who had a girlfriend. Some of my dreams were mere *flavors of the month.* Others have stayed with me throughout my life.

One of my dreams has always been to find *the One.* I wasn't looking for the character *Neo* from the movie *The Matrix.* I was dreaming of someone to spend my life with. You know what I'm talking about. I wanted someone to *share* my life with: a special someone who I could laugh with, someone I could explore the world with. That unique person who would love me for who I am and be there to put my teeth back in when I grow old.

I could be with anyone, but I was looking to spend my life with someone. I often wondered who that someone would be. I didn't sit around waiting for them to appear out of the blue. I had a life to live. I knew that I wasn't going to meet them sitting on my couch.

"Fresh from the Kitchen"

In the previous chapter, I stated how every person or experience in our life is a puzzle piece of our grand vision. My sister-in-law Kathleen Duran is one of my puzzle pieces. She is the older sister of my wife Kelly. I met her in Las Vegas in 2004. I was in town celebrating my birthday with my friends. We were at the *Bellagio Hotel and Resort* celebrating and dancing the night away. During the festivities, I noticed Kathleen being harassed. I didn't know her at the time, but I did understand her body language. She and her friend Melissa were being hit on by a man who didn't understand the phrase "we're not interested." I approached and asked her if they needed help. They told the man: "we're with them." The ladies thanked us for helping them. They remarked about how our group looked like we were having fun. I told them how several of us were in town to celebrate our birthdays.

Kathleen and Melissa hung out with our group long enough to learn a few dance steps before they left. Being guys, my friends asked, "did you get their phone numbers?" You could see the disappointment on their faces when I answered with a "no." They razzed me, and we continued our night. I could have kicked myself for not getting their information. The little voice in my head told me that I should have asked for their phone numbers. About an hour later, the ladies returned. They informed us of how our group was fun and they would like to hang out with us some more. I was given a second chance. The night ended with an exchange of business cards and an invitation to hang out with the ladies the following day.

"Fresh from the Kitchen"

The next day, I called the number on the card. My friends and I were invited to a pool party at the *Monte Carlo* hotel. I asked my friends who wanted to go, but they all declined with a lot of stupid excuses. I decided to go... by myself. The pool party and day with the ladies was a good time. We spent some time by the pool having lunch and visited a couple of shops on the strip. My new friends asked me to keep in touch and I promised that I would. I thanked them for a good time and continued to vacation with my friends.

Six months later, I was in Las Vegas again with my best friend Scott. Melissa and Kathleen were in town, too. I had kept in touch with them through email. We arranged to meet for lunch. Melissa was working at a convention, so we hung out with just Kathleen. This time we had lunch poolside at the *Mandalay Bay Hotel and Resort.* We talked about Las Vegas, how we met, my pursuit of speaking career, and my dating life. I had just ended a relationship and was just looking to spend time with friends and family. Lunch ended and we thanked Kathleen for spending time with us.

When I returned from my vacation, I received an email from Kathleen. She thanked Scott and I for spending time with her while Melissa was busy. She also suggested that I meet her sister. She felt that we had a lot in common, and that we would hit it off. Never doubt a woman's intuition. Kathleen spent the next several months telling me everything about her sister Kelly. I was flattered by Kathleen's trust in me, but I lived over 2,000 miles away from her sister.

"Fresh from the Kitchen"

After months of friendly suggestions, I finally contacted Kelly. Kathleen had sent me her email and phone number. We didn't hit it off instantly, but we had a good conversations. Over the next year, Kelly and I developed a friendship. The friendship developed into dating after I met her. Dating became a serious relationship. The serious relationship made me move across the country to live with Kelly. The next step was for me to drop down on one knee and propose to Kelly. A year after the proposal, we were married. During the reception of October 16, 2010, Kathleen talked about how we met during her toast. She talked about one of her dreams. The dream that Kelly and I would be together. I thanked her in front of family and friends. I'm also thanking her in this book.

Make the most out of every opportunity and experience. You never know how it could affect your life. Life is a jigsaw puzzle. Every experience and relationship is a piece to that puzzle. You may not recognize how that piece fits the puzzle right away, but eventually, you will. Kathleen is a piece to my puzzle and I am a piece of hers. A random act of kindness can go a long way. That is why I have thanked Kathleen for her suggestion several times. I owe her a lifetime more.

Thank you Kathleen. My puzzle would be incomplete without you and your sister!

Lesson 38

"Pursue your Passions not Jobs!"

"I can't imagine anything more worthwhile than doing what I love most. And they pay me for it." – Edgar Winter

"Hi. My name is Frank C. Kitchen and my initials say it all. You should hire me because I am fun, creative, and knowledgeable. I create the environment that everyone desires to work in. If you need someone to plan your next event, train your staff, or motivate your employees, then contact me at hirefrankkitchen@yahoo.com. That's H-I- R-E Frank Kitchen, like the room, at Yahoo.com. No job is too big or too small. All I need is you and the opportunity to shine."

Those are the words I spoke on January 28, 2010. I was appearing on the cable news network *CNN.* I was a guest on *30 Second Pitch.* I had 30 seconds to tell the world on live television why I would be a great employee. After my appearance, I received emails from around the world. I received compliments. People thanked me for inspiring them. I also received offers for a variety of *pyramid schemes*. The one thing that I didn't receive was a legitimate job offer. I thought that the job offers would overwhelm me. I had nailed my live interview, but I was still looking for a job. That day made me realize that I am not defined by a job.

"Fresh from the Kitchen"

Jobs, careers, and work that you pursue have a huge impact on your dreams. In 2007, I left my job at Lakeland Community College to pursue my passion. I was going to be a full-time professional speaker. I had saved my money. Contracted work was lined up. I was moving across the country to live with my future wife. Everything was going great until *The World Financial Crisis* hit. People were losing jobs, companies were filing for bankruptcy, and everyone was cutting their budgets. Not a good time to start a new business as a speaker.

My adventures as a professional job hunter began in 2008. My speaking calendar was very inconsistent. I was under-employed. I was working, but not enough to pay my bills. I figured that it would be easy for me to get a job to help make ends meet. I was armed with a great resume, a killer personality, a college degree, and a long list of accomplishments. I expected a great paying job with lots of responsibility.

I read countless articles about the changing job environment. The articles said that I shouldn't let my ego or pride get in the way of my job hunt. So, I applied for everything.

Here are a few of the jobs I applied for:

Painter, substitute teacher, toxic waste disposal, bank teller, event planner, product representative, solar sales, water sales, flight attendant, rental car sales associate, stadium tour guide, security officer, school crossing guard, street sweeper, personal trainer, audio and visual technician, hot air balloon employee, apartment rentals, youth mentor, human resources positions, speakers series director, zoo employee, sports league coordinator, secretary, office manager, youth mentor, personal assistant, pharmaceutical representative, acting coach, model coach, volunteer trainer, Student Activities Director, hotel manager, movie theatre employee, waiter, public address announcer, pizza cook, valet, limo driver, delivery man, writer, golf course attendant, radio station representative, census worker, fundraiser, telemarketer, hospital baby photographer, birthday party host, and as a speaker.

I was turned down for every job above. No interviews, no decline letters, and no reason for why I wasn't good enough. I am a very confident individual, but my confidence was starting to wane. I was a National Keynote speaker, but was being turned down for *9-5 jobs*. I could train a company's employees at a conference one day. The next day, I would be turned down for a job as a corporate trainer. Why couldn't I get a job? Why couldn't I get an interview? Why couldn't I get a simple letter saying, "thanks, but no thanks"? I was no longer living the American Dream. I was living the American Nightmare. I was waking up to *The Employment Hustle.*

The Employment Hustle is what job hunters are experiencing everywhere. It's just like a board game. This board game has a major problem. There are numerous players, but only one player has the rules. That one player has the ability to change the rules anytime they want.

That one player is known as *The Employer*. The only way for you to win this game is to learn the tricks of the trade. You have to learn that your job is not your life.

You are not defined by your job. You are defined by your passions, pursuits, beliefs, and accomplishments. A job is a tool used to accomplish your dreams. When you start to think this way, you will be one step closer to living your dreams.

I applied for every job under the sun. It was the wrong thing to do. I wasn't getting any closer to my dreams. I was desperate. Don't chase after the hot jobs listed on a website. Don't follow trends blindly. Don't listen to the people who say there is a *right way* to write a resume. You will find job fairs that don't have jobs. Job hunting is subjective. Employers have the upper hand because there are millions of people willing to work for anything. You have to pursue work that you are passionate about and allow you to showcase your talents.

When you pursue a passion, it's not work. My best friend Scott is a golf coach. He loves to play golf. It's an expensive sport, but it's a passion. His father first taught him the game that he fell in love with. His dream is to play as much as possible and be the best that he can. To accomplish his dream, he started working at a golf course and coaching the local high school golf team. Both jobs allow him the opportunity to play all the golf he wants. It equates to thousands of dollars saved. He has truly worked to create a lifestyle. Scott is not simply working, he is living his dream. You have to work to create the lifestyle that you want.

"Fresh from the Kitchen"

The best work opportunity for you isn't always posted on a jobsite. You have to go out and create it.

"The single greatest error and deception of our accounting system: people are paced in the liability column on the balance sheet. Machinery and computers are categorized as assets and people as liabilities." – The Dream Manager by Matthew Kelly

You are not guaranteed a job. I thought that I was. I learned that an employer doesn't have to hire you. Personnel costs are the greatest expenditure for any business. Companies are cutting costs and trying to improve profits. They can layoff employees with a snap of their fingers.

They can choose not to hire new staff when the costs are too expensive. You are seen as a liability. As a liability, you have to prove how you will help the employer build their dream or prove that you can make them money. For every job opening, there are several qualified candidates and hundreds of prospective candidates applying for the position that you want. A company is loyal to its stockholders and that is the bottom line. They don't have to give you a job. You can no longer expect to have a job. You have to earn it. During your job hunts, find employers to work with, not work *for*. When you work with someone, it's a partnership. You're working together to help build each other's dreams.

"Fresh from the Kitchen"

Scott created his opportunities. He befriended the right people and let them know about his passion for golf. Scott learned about his golfing jobs by networking. The United States Labor Department stated that 69% of job hunters acquired their jobs through networking or talking to someone that they know.

Don't spend all of your valuable time searching job websites. The sites don't allow you to stand out from the crowd. Talk to the people that you know. These people know you well. They can give you a recommendation that a website can't. If 69% of employment comes from knowing someone, why do people spend the majority of their time seeking employment from people they don't know? Focus your valuable time and energy on the people who care about you.

Nothing is guaranteed. The chances of you being with a company for life are slim. Don't base your life around your work. Pursue work where you will have more positive experiences than negative. Find an environment that you desire to work in. Take advantage of the job, and don't let it take advantage of you. Find work that allows you to use your special skills and talents. Find work that assists you with living your dreams. Pursue a passion. When you are passionate about something, it's not a job – you are hiring yourself to live your life.

Lesson 39

"It's Better to be Respected than Liked."

"The story you are about to read is true. Only the names have been changed to protect the innocent." – 1950s Television show, Dragnet

Not everyone is going to like you in life. It's the truth I share with leaders around the world. Someone may not like the way you look, another person may not like how you act. Others may not like the way you do things. A few may not like you because they are jealous of your abilities. It is their prerogative, but do they respect you?

I was working at the *African Wildlife Park* performing the *Animal Adventure* talk. I was talking to a large crowd about our African elephants. I was giving fun facts and stories about our family of five. During the talks, I handed out carrots to the crowd. They threw the carrots into the exhibit to help feed the elephants. It was a great experience for the little kids and the big kids. When I say big kids, I mean the adults.

I always told the crowds to respect the elephants by not throwing the carrots in their pond, hitting the elephants with the carrots, or yelling at them.

"Fresh from the Kitchen"

During the talk, the elephant named Peanut started to walk away. I wanted him to come closer to the crowd. I tossed a couple of carrots in front of him in hopes he would come over to eat them. That didn't work, so I tried talking to him. I said, "come here Peanut, the people want to see you." Then, I made a large swinging motion with my right arm, the motion you would make when you're trying to get someone to come towards you. He came over and waved his trunk up and down; he didn't look happy. That was very unusual for Peanut, so I spoke to some co-workers after the talk. I asked if I had done something wrong. I asked if I had upset the elephant.

Word quickly spread around the wildlife park that I had upset Peanut. Co-workers were teasing me that I had pissed off the elephants. They joked about what other animals at the park I could upset. I asked, "Does Peanut hate me?"

I was worried, so my friend Penny talked to the elephant keepers. She told me, "the elephant doesn't like you." What did that mean? The elephant didn't like me? Did he not like my voice? Did he not like other men? Did he not like the color of my skin? Was the elephant racist? Was I going to lose my job for upsetting the elephant?

Seeing the look on my face, Penny smiled and told me she was joking. She told me that my hand gesture could have signaled Peanut to raise his trunk. He had been a part of a circus before coming to the wildlife park. His former trainers may have taught him the trunk motion.

I was relieved, but still had months of jokes to endure. I did play a few jokes on my own. I told my one coworker that I couldn't work around the elephants because they didn't like me. Pete listened to the full story as I explained my fears. Being a concerned individual, Pete told me he was going to get some answers. That's when I told him the truth. He laughed.

I talked to the keepers and asked what I should and shouldn't do around the elephants. They explained that animals are just like people. They have personalities. They have good days and not so good days. Peanut just wasn't in the mood for carrots that day.

Life isn't about having someone or something like you. Life is about earning the respect of an individual or group. No one wants to be disliked. I spent days trying to find out if an elephant didn't like me. I should have done more to learn more about the elephants. You earn respect when you practice what you preach and live up to your promises. You earn respect from others when you take the time to learn about them. You learn their personalities. You discover their likes and dislikes. You take the time to truly understand their motivations and passions. People spend too much time trying to motivate others to like them. It is nice to be liked, but it's better to be respected.

Lesson 40

"Be Contagious...Positively Contagious!"

"Everyday we have over 10,000 interactions! We need 5 positive interactions to negate every negative interaction."
– How Full is Your Bucket, 2004

Every day, you have the opportunity to make a choice. You can choose to do something positive.Or you can choose to do something negative. The choice can affect the life of someone else in a positive or negative way. If a rotten apple can spoil the bunch, what happens with a positive apple? Positivity and Negativity are contagious.

Many of my experiences working at the Phoenix Zoo could fill an entire book. My adventure with the "floating sandal" is one that is worth sharing in this book.

I worked as an Experience Guide at the zoo. The position required me to interact with guests all day. My brain and body were always happy when my work shifts ended. One evening, I was taking the long walk to the employee break room and time clock. I was walking with my co-worker, Kelly. We talked about the long and tiring day. We couldn't wait to get home.

"Fresh from the Kitchen"

As we passed the elephant exhibit, we noticed a child limping. The little girl was with her parents and younger brother. I looked at her feet and noticed that she was missing a sandal.

I asked her, "what happened to your sandal?" In tears she responded, "It's in the lake." The girl's parents told us that the sandal was in the lake near the Children's Trail and would be impossible to get.

Seeing the little girl in tears, we felt it was worth an attempt to find the sandal. The girl wouldn't stop crying. We pulled out our radios and called for an available zookeeper. We would need a boat to retrieve the sandal. Kelly had a very important event to get to, so I told her I would assist the family. The family followed me to the trail. I asked the girl how her sandal got in the lake. I really couldn't decipher what she was saying between the crying, sniffling, and deep breaths. Her brother said, "the sandal is floating in the lake near the monkeys."

This sounded easy. Just find the sandal floating near the monkeys. All we would need is a boat from a keeper and something to scoop it up. We arrived at the bridge near the monkeys. The boy yelled out: "there it is!"

The sandal was there. It was floating in the green algae on the opposite side of the monkey's lake. Every zoo employee knew this area was full of cattails and mud deep enough to swallow anyone whole.

"Fresh from the Kitchen"

The good news was that the sandal was floating a mere ten feet from the shore. The bad news was that it was about ten feet from the shore. Tangled palm fronds and floating debris would make this a tough catch.

The girl's parents told me not to worry about it, but I really thought that I could get it. That's when one of the keepers, Cat, arrived. I explained to her what had happened and asked for a long rake. As she handed it to me, she reminded me to be careful.

With my rake in hand, I headed down to the shoreline to fish out the sandal. It was more of an embankment, a very wet embankment with terrible footing. What I thought was solid ground was actually floating debris. My left foot slid into the water and got more than a little wet. This is when the Cat told me, "don't fall in the water!"

The rake wasn't long enough, but I couldn't give up. Again, the parents told us not to worry about it and that we had done enough. That's when we noticed a long palm branch near the shore. It was just the right length to reach the sandal.

From a safe and dry spot, I was able to use the end of the branch to drag the sandal closer to shore. When it got closer, I used the rake to fish out the sandal. Victoriously, I cried out that I found the sandal. I turned to see the little girl and her mother displaying big smiles. I returned the sandal to its proper owner.

Cat pointed the family to the nearest restroom and recommended they wash the sandal off. The parents thanked us for all of our help and walked toward the restroom.

With one soggy shoe and one dry shoe, I arrived at the time clock. My manager asked about my radio calls. I explained the details of my mission to return Cinderella's slipper. My manager told me, "Nice job, but you didn't have to do that."

On my first day of training, I was told we needed to do "wild" things to make our zoo guests happy. The sandal may not be important to a lot of people, but it was important to the little girl. She wasn't happy on her way out the first time, but by the time we got her sandal out of the water, she and her family were happy. The experience made me feel really good inside as I drove home. I got to share my positive energy. I know that positive experience made the family feel good about the Phoenix Zoo and the people who work there.

Lesson 41

“You Define Your Success!”

"Success isn't just about what you accomplish in your life; it's about what you inspire others to do.” -Unknown

I'm not world famous. I've never made $1 million. I'm not a professional athlete. I didn't graduate at the top of my class. I'm skinny. I have college debt. I don't have a big house. I don't own a fancy car. I’ve been fired several times. I’ve experienced numerous failures. You’ve probably found a typo in this book. After reading that list, many people would say that I'm not successful. I'd tell those people they are wrong!

We live in a culture and time where success is judged by what you have. Society is very materialistic. If you're "rich" you're a success. The funny thing is, many of the "rich" people we admire are broke. Broke mentally, broke physically, broke spiritually and many times broke fiscally too. Our culture tells us to think negatively of ourselves if we don't possess the latest and the greatest. People put others down based on what they have versus who they are.

I'm sure you're asking where is Frank going with this? Here's where I'm going. I define success as achieving or living your dream. All of our dreams don't involve owning something.

I may not be rich or famous, but I have had a positive influence on thousands of people. That's one of my dreams, that makes me a success. I dreamed of having a college degree. I was 30 years old when I finally earned it, that makes me a success. I wanted to visit Australia. I was able to visit Australia by volunteering with Rotary International. I get to spend quality time with my wife and children. All successes.

That list is just a few of the things I wrote on my "grocery list" of things I have dreamed of doing. Every time I cross something off of that list, I'm a success.

We live in a very judgmental world. One that judges us on things that really don't matter. The next time you wonder if you're a success, remember all of the dreams you have accomplished and look forward to all of the dreams you will still achieve.

Lesson 42

"You may have to Work for Yourself to Live Your Dreams."

"Some people are born to work for people and others are born to work with people."
- Frank Kitchen

For years I had people suggest that I should be an entrepreneur or business owner. After years of working various jobs for good bosses and bad, I realized they were right. I was born to work with people not for people. When I'm invited to coach entrepreneurs and prospective entrepreneurs, I challenge them with the following questions. Being an Entrepreneur/ Business Owner can be very rewarding, but also requires a lot of work, dedication, and sacrifice. If you can't answer yes to all or most of these questions, you are limiting and preventing your success as a business owner.

Can you spell entrepreneur?

- To be successful at something you must be able to spell it.

Are you doing something daily to grow your business or grow yourself as a business person?

- On a daily basis, you should be working to grow your business. Actual business work, talking with other business owners, reading articles, listening to podcasts or audiobooks and studying your craft.

I don't wait for people to tell you what to do? I am self-motivated!

- WAIT = Wish An Idea Turns out. Entrepreneurship is a proactive activity. If people have to tell you to do something, then you really don't want to be successful. You must successful people in the world ask questions. Always Seek Knowledge. ASK for help, ASK for solutions and ASK. You must push yourself.

- The perfect time to start something is right now. Brainstorm, write a plan, read, study, join a Facebook or LinkedIn group, take a class, block out time in your calendar. The more you wait, the longer things will take.

I don't treat my business as a hobby!

"Are you treating your dream (business) like a hobby?" - Kelly Duran

- A business isn't a hobby. Hobbies don't get you paid or keep the lights on. Are you treating your business like your child? (Showing it love, respect and dedicating your time, talent, team, and treasures to help it grow) A business needs attention and nourishment.

Are you producing more than you consume?

- Entrepreneurs are business owners. Businesses produce content, services, and products for consumers. Producers create opportunities for themselves and others to grow. Consumers are dependent on others to grow.

Are you investing more time in things that don't help you grow personally or professionally?

- How do you invest your time? It's ok to read and do fun stuff, but if you do more fun stuff than stuff that will help you have fun your business is in trouble.
- If you can't invest even 10 minutes a day to grow your business or yourself, then your business isn't important to you.

You're not afraid to fail?

- Entrepreneurship is a series of failures you will learn from. If you're afraid to fail, then your business will fail.
- To avoid major failures, learn from the failures of others. When you meet a successful entrepreneur ask them about their failures, not their successes.

Are you willing to sacrifice?

- What will you sacrifice short term or long term to have a successful business? Television, Social Media, Partying, Material items or Free Time. Success takes dedication and discipline. You can't have everything, so you must figure out what you want more? What are you willing to give up to get what you want?

Does your community know you are a business owner?

- The first person you must sell on anything is yourself. If you don't think of yourself as a business owner (the person responsible for the well being and survival of your business) then your community of friends, family and potential customers won't think of you as a business owner either. It all starts with you.

Do you know your business inside and out?

- The idea of owning your own business sounds like fun, but it takes dedication and discipline. You must know the who, what, when, how and why of your business. Everything to make it flourish. When you don't know your business, it will fail. You must push yourself to know how everything works, so you'll know what is needed for it to be successful. You can ask others to assist or help you when you don't understand that you need help.

Lesson 43

"Stop Holding Yourself Back!"

"Get busy living, or get busy dying."
- Shawshank Redemption 1994

The quote above is from one of my favorite movies, "Shawshank Redemption." I liked the movie so much, I used to practice lines from the movie in my acting classes. One of my favorite lines is above.

Have you ever caught yourself saying, "this is not how my life is supposed to be!" Have you ever blamed others for your life? This is what our society has become. We lack personal responsibility. We blame someone else when we aren't living our dreams. I'll admit it, my mind has gone there more than a few times. That's when I realized the person most responsible for me from living life is me!

Getting the full experience of life, and all it has to offer starts with you. It's about what you do and what you stop doing!

I know what you're asking, "What do you do to live life to the fullest?" My simple answer is this. You have to stop doing the 5 things below. When I Stopped Lying...Stopped Trying...Stopped Caring...Stopped Worrying...and Stopped Waiting, my life as a husband, father, friend and entrepreneur changed dramatically.

#1 Stop Lying!

You have dreams, some come true and others don't. Why aren't your dreams coming true? Why aren't you living them? Do you make excuses when they don't become reality? Do you blame other people? Stop lying to yourself! When you don't live your dreams, you get angry, depressed and start to doubt yourself. You lie to make yourself feel better. You lie to protect yourself. You lie to justify why your dreams aren't coming true. The truth is, every time you lie (I'm too old, too poor, not educated enough, not pretty enough…), you are preventing yourself from living life.

It's one thing to lie to other people, but when you lie to yourself, you are hurting yourself. You are killing your dream. If you are not achieving the dreams you want to live, you need to be honest with yourself. You have to change your thinking. You can't blame other people, you must take personal responsibility. You have to ask yourself are you doing what it takes to make your dreams come true. You need to set a goal. You need to make a plan. You need to follow through on your plan. You MUST BE HONEST with yourself and others.

#2 Stop Trying!

What are your dreams? What do you want to do? Don't live the dreams of someone else. Live Your Dreams. Don't try to be someone else. It's hard enough being you. Be yourself. Stop trying to be something that you're not.

Don't be the next (Insert Name Here), be the next you! The best you possible. People spend too much time trying to be something they're not. I love what Yoda says in *The Empire Strikes Back,* "Do or do not, there is no try."

What makes you happy? Why do these activities make you happy? Write those thoughts down, make them into goals, put together a plan to make them happen and go out and do what it takes to make them happen! Talk about what you WILL DO versus what you will try.

#3 Stop Caring!

What do YOU care about? Who truly cares about YOU? Stop caring about the thoughts and opinions of people who don't care about you and your dreams. This doesn't mean you surround yourself with a bunch of "YES PEOPLE." You want to be around people who truly CARE for you and your dreams. People who COMMUNICATE, APPRECIATE, RESPECT and EDUCATE YOU.

People spend too much time worrying about the thoughts and opinions of people who don't CARE about them or their dreams. You need to CARE about the opinions of the people who truly CARE about you and your well being.

#4 Stop Worrying!

Once you stop caring, you can stop worrying too! Stop worrying about things you can't control. Worry about the things you can control. You can't change the weather, but you can decide the appropriate clothing to wear for the weather. You can check the weather report. You can stay inside or go out.

When you worry about things you can't control, you become stagnant. Your worries paralyze you. Your worries prevent your dreams from coming true. Worry more about what you can do, versus what you can't do. Worry more about what can go right versus what can go wrong. Worry about what you can control.

Worries are Fears. FEAR is FALSE EVIDENCE APPEARING REAL. When you worry about what you can control, you are doing research. You are searching for the truth. You are focusing on what is possible. You are mentally pointing yourself in the right direction.

#5 Stop Waiting!

I hear people say "I hope this happens." "I'll get to it tomorrow." "When "X" happens, then I'll do "Y"! "My dream will never come true." "I don't have the time." "I don't have enough money." "People will laugh at me." "I'll try another time."

Tomorrow isn't guaranteed. All of the excuses above are made by people waiting for something to happen. The main difference between people who successfully achieve their dreams and people who don't...the successful people take the necessary actions to make things happen, they don't wait for things to happen.

When your dreams are truly important to you, you will show a sense of urgency. The dream doesn't have to come true right now, but you can start working on it right now. Whether you start writing down your dreams; you share your dream with a friend; you make a plan; or you do research on your dream, you are not waiting, you are doing.

Be a person of action. Make your dreams come true. Be honest with yourself, be yourself, seek out the support and advice from people who care about you, don't let your worries stop you and make things happen. **The more you dream about your dreams, they further away they get!**

Lesson 44

"Live F.R.E.S.H.!"

"A Dream you only talk about becomes a Fantasy.
A Dream you work to Live becomes a Reality!"
– Frank Kitchen

Congratulations! You've come to the last chapter of the book.

I truly hope the lessons shared in this book provide you with the knowledge and encouragement to transform your big dreams into a reality. Your big dreams are the dreams you hunger for and keep you up at night.

Every lesson I have shared with you in this book was written to get you one step closer to being the person who is known for living the dreams they hunger for. I want you to Live Focused, Resourceful, Enthusiastic, Strong and Honest. This is your recipe for being a Positive Difference Maker and Life Changer in your community, organization or workplace. This is Living F.R.E.S.H.!

When you commit your time, talent, team and treasures to living your dreams while helping others live their dreams; You impact a person's life in a positive way. Here is my five part recipe for creating a mindset that allows you to cook up the tasty results others will attempt to replicate.

Focus

To live your big dreams you need to avoid distractions. You must focus on what you will do to transform your dreams into a reality. Be very specific with your focus. When do you want to live your dream? Where do you want to live your dream? How do you want to live your dream? Who do you want to live your dream with? Why do you want to live your dream?

The more specific and focused you are, the closer you will be to living your dreams.

Resourceful

To live your big dreams you need to be resourceful. You have to figure out the resources you have and the resources you will need to acquire. When you don't possess the skills, knowledge, finances or physical resources you need; get creative and find a way to obtain what you need. Reach out to people you know and develop relationships with people you don't know.

Enthusiastic

To live your big dreams you must be enthusiastic about them. You must show a passion, desire and commitment to transform your dream into a reality. You have to be positive. You have to think about what you can do, not what you can't do. You have to bring a can do mindset. No enthusiasm, no reality.

Strong

To live the your big dreams, you must be strong. Tough times are going to happen, you must stay mentally strong. Strength is something you build and develop. Are you connecting with people who are mentally strong or mentally weak? Where the mind goes the body will follow. You have to believe in what you're doing. You must have a detailed plan on how you will turn your vision into reality. Where your mind goes, your body will follow.

Honest

To live your big dreams, you need to be honest. You need to be honest with the people around you, but most importantly, you need to be honest with yourself. You need to look in the mirror and admit that you can't do everything by yourself. You need to ask for assistance. You need to admit when you're wrong. You need to admit your failures and areas you can improve. You need to admit why you are pursuing your dream. When you lie your dreams become a fantasy instead of reality.

When you Live *FRESH,* you possess a mindset to live a life that is exciting, appealing and rewarding for you and others. You are living a life where dreams flourish. I want to thank you for making the time to read this book and make one of my big dreams flourish. I'd love to hear about the dreams you are pursuing and the dreams that you have cooked up.

Frank

ABOUT THE AUTHOR

Frank Kitchen is the "Mindset Master Chef." He is a Fundraiser, Coach, and Keynote Speaker. For over 25 years, he has worked with Professional Associations, Businesses, Non-Profits, and Schools to teach their leaders, members, staff, students, and volunteers to breakthrough mental barriers to cook up the dreams they hunger for. His Keynote Speeches, Educational Workshops, and Coaching Programs have taught leaders and their teams how to commit their time, talents, teams and treasures to produce positive results for themselves and others by implementing his " I Live F.R.E.S.H." Recipe. His recipe is the same plan he practices to raise millions of dollars annually for nonprofits as one of the first African American Fundraising Auctioneers in the world.

Born in Bad Kreuznach, Germany, he grew up as a "military brat." His family constantly relocated around the world during his childhood. The continuous travel provided diverse life experiences. Their travels taught him about leadership and gave me visual examples of what life has to offer.

His leadership journey began in college when he served as a student leader to help pay for my education. I was elected to represent my fellow students as a Student Government Officer.

That experience led him and several classmates to start the Lakeland Community College Campus Activities Board where he was elected as the organization's first President. His college student leadership experience led him to earn an Associate of Arts Degree from Lakeland Community College (Ohio) and a Bachelor of Science Degree in Business Administration from David N. Myers College (Ohio).

The leadership knowledge and skills he gained in college created multiple supervisory opportunities with employers including a position as an award-winning Toy Store Manager and Trainer for KB Toys. His passion for servant leadership led him back to Lakeland Community College as the Assistant Director of Student Activities where he specialized in leadership development, diversity programming, and event facilitation.

Teaching students and professionals how to lead themselves and others was a very fulfilling career choice that he thought would last a lifetime. For years he challenged his students to live their personal and professional dreams. This inspired them to challenge Frank. They encouraged him to leave my stable college position to pursue the unpredictable career of professional speaker/entrepreneur. They wanted him to share his knowledge and experience with a global audience.

Frank has been blessed to share his tactics and strategies on effective leadership all around the world.

When he isn't speaking, Frank pursues his passion for servant leadership by exploring the world with his wife and two children; volunteering as a mentor for aspiring entrepreneurs; and raising money and awareness for philanthropic causes as a fundraising ambassador, and auctioneer. Not bad for a dreamer who got involved in Leadership for a t-shirt, a trip and the opportunity to make a difference!

Please contact Frank Kitchen Enterprises, to learn how Frank can partner with you and your organization to make your next Conference, Convention, Retreat, Orientation, Fundraiser, or Training Event a F.R.E.S.H. Experience.

www.FRANKKITCHEN.com
480-405-7658 (Office Line)
FRESH@FRANKKITCHEN.COM

Social Media
Twitter / Instagram / Youtube / LinkedIn
@FrankKitchen

Made in the USA
Middletown, DE
30 April 2022